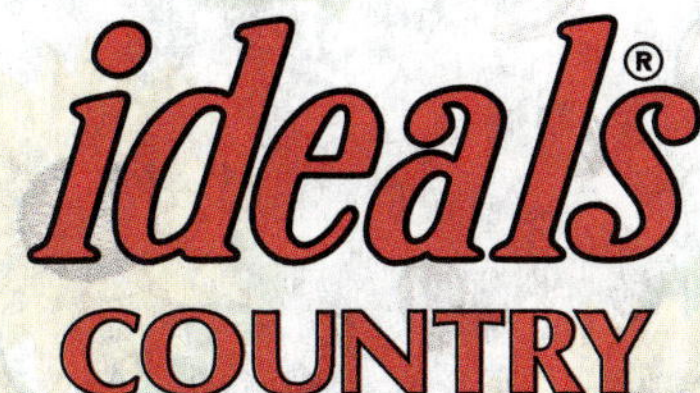

More Than 50 Years of Celebrating Life's Most Treasured Moments

Vol. 59, No. 3

Beyond my heart I need not reach
when all is summer there.
—John Vance Cheney

IDEALS—Vol. 59, No. 3 May MMII IDEALS (ISSN 0019-137X, USPS 256-240)
is published six times a year: January, March, May, July, September, and November by
IDEALS PUBLICATIONS, a division of Guideposts
39 Seminary Hill Road, Carmel, NY 10512.

Title IDEALS registered U.S. Patent Office. Printed and bound in USA by Quebecor Printing.

Printed on Weyerhaeuser Husky. The paper used in this publication meets the minimum requirements of
American National Standard for Information Sciences—
Permanence of Paper for Printed Library Materials, ANSI Z39.48-1984.

Periodicals postage paid at Carmel, New York, and additional mailing offices.
POSTMASTER: Send address changes to Ideals, 39 Seminary Hill Road, Carmel, NY 10512.
For subscription or customer service questions, contact Ideals Publications,
a division of Guideposts, 39 Seminary Hill Road, Carmel, NY 10512. Fax 845-228-2115.

Reader Preference Service: We occasionally make our mailing lists available to
other companies whose products or services might interest you.
If you prefer not to be included, please write to Ideals Customer Service.

ISBN 0-8249-1201-2 GST 893989236

Visit *Ideals'* website at www.idealsbooks.com

Cover Photo: Colonial home in Strasburg, Pennsylvania. Photo by Larry Lefever/Grant Heilman Photography.
Inside Front Cover: PICNIC. *Mary Kay Krell, artist.*
Inside Back Cover: THE YOUNG ANGLERS. *James Hardy, Jr., artist.*
Roy Miles Gallery, 29 Bruton Street, London W1/Bridgeman Art Library, London/Superstock.

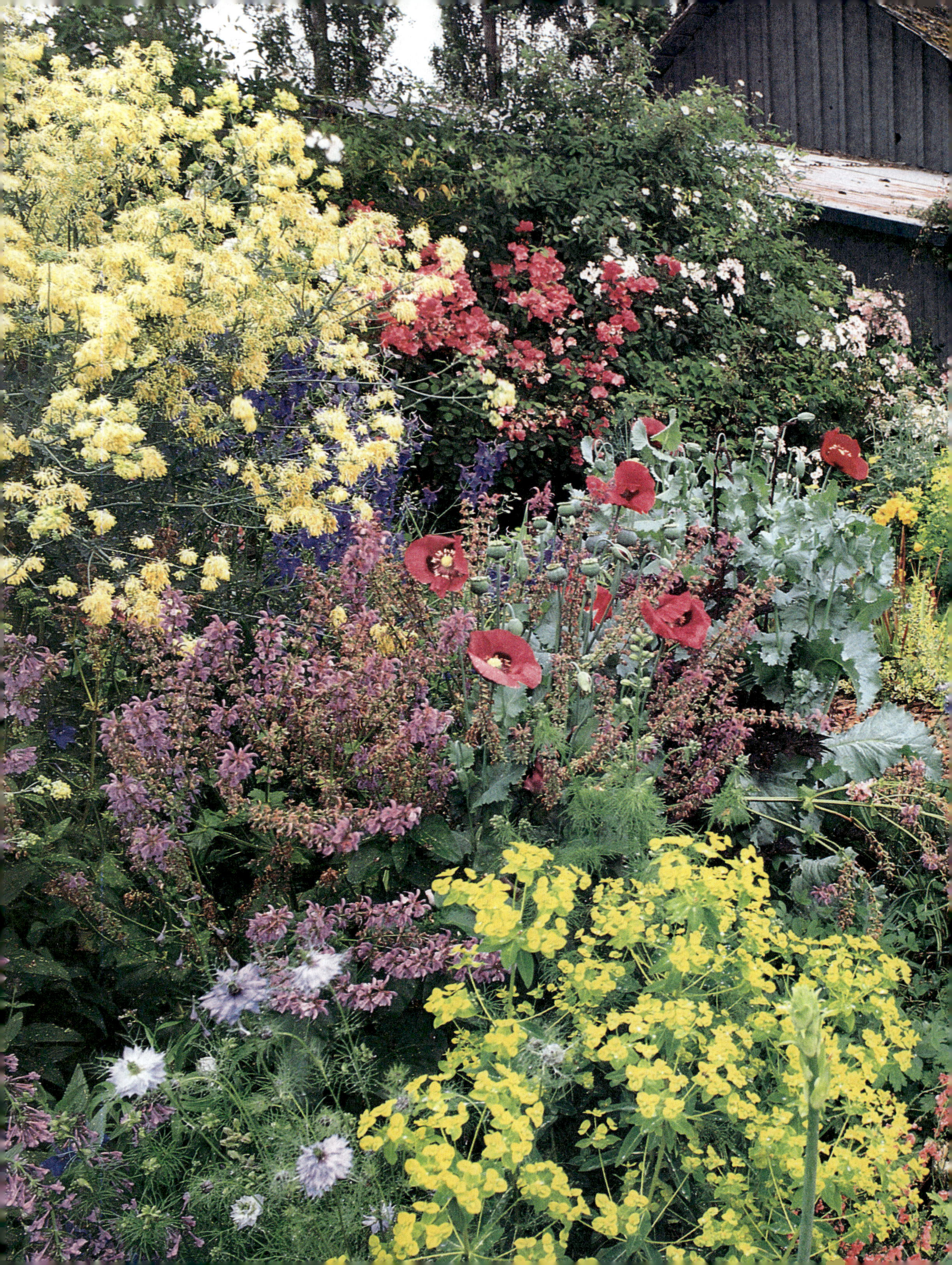

Ideals brings you the fascinating History of the Bible . . .

Now, the story of the writing, the preservation, and the translations of the world's most beloved and powerful book is told in an exquisitely illustrated volume entitled—*The Story of the Bible.*

Within the pages of this magnificent volume, you'll discover how the words of the Bible were preserved—from early Hebrew texts of the Old Testament to the letters and manuscripts of the New Testament. You'll understand why the sixty-six books of the Bible have remained the Word of God and why other manuscripts were rejected.

The Story of The Bible

By Patricia A. Pingry

Words of Wisdom from the Bible

FREE WORDS OF WISDOM BOOKLET JUST FOR ORDERING

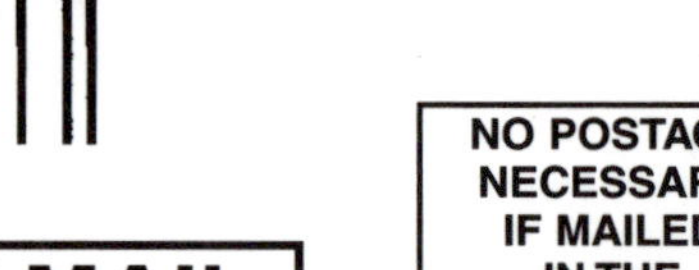

NO POSTAGE NECESSARY IF MAILED IN THE UNITED STATES

BUSINESS REPLY MAIL
FIRST-CLASS MAIL PERMIT NO. 38 CARMEL NY

POSTAGE WILL BE PAID BY ADDRESSEE

GUIDEPOSTS
PO BOX 797
CARMEL NY 10512-9905

You'll also receive fresh insight into:

* The four Gospels, the men who wrote them, and how the texts were preserved throughout the years.
* The Old Testament scribes, such as Baruch, who risked his own life to keep a record of the prophecies of Jeremiah.
* The monks who painstakingly copied the ancient texts, often illuminating the pages with an artistic beauty.
* William Tyndale, whose English translation was the first Bible printed but who was also executed for his work.
* The English translation authorized by King James I, completed in 1611, which remains the most revered Bible of all time.
* Discoveries still being made of pieces of original scrolls, letters, and documents that amazingly correspond to our printed Bible.

Return the Free Examination Certificate today to preview *The Story of the Bible* for 30 days FREE . . . and receive FREE *Words of Wisdom* booklet just for ordering.

FREE EXAMINATION CERTIFICATE

YES! I'd like to examine *The Story of the Bible* for 30 days FREE. If after 30 days I am not delighted with it, I may return it and owe nothing. If I decide to keep it, I will be billed $24.95, plus postage and handling. In either case, the FREE *Words of Wisdom* booklet is mine to keep.

Please print your name and address:

MY NAME ______________________

MY ADDRESS ______________________

CITY ______________ STATE ________ ZIP ________

Total copies ordered __________

❏ Please Bill Me ❏ Charge My: ❏ MasterCard ❏ Visa

Credit Card #: ☐☐☐☐ ☐☐☐☐ ☐☐☐☐ ☐☐☐☐

Expiration Date: ______________

Signature ______________

Allow 4 weeks for delivery. Orders subject to credit approval.
Send no money now. We will bill you later.
www.IdealsBooks.com

015/201870161

Complete the Free Examinatio[n] Certificate and mail today for your 30-Day Preview.

No need to send money now!

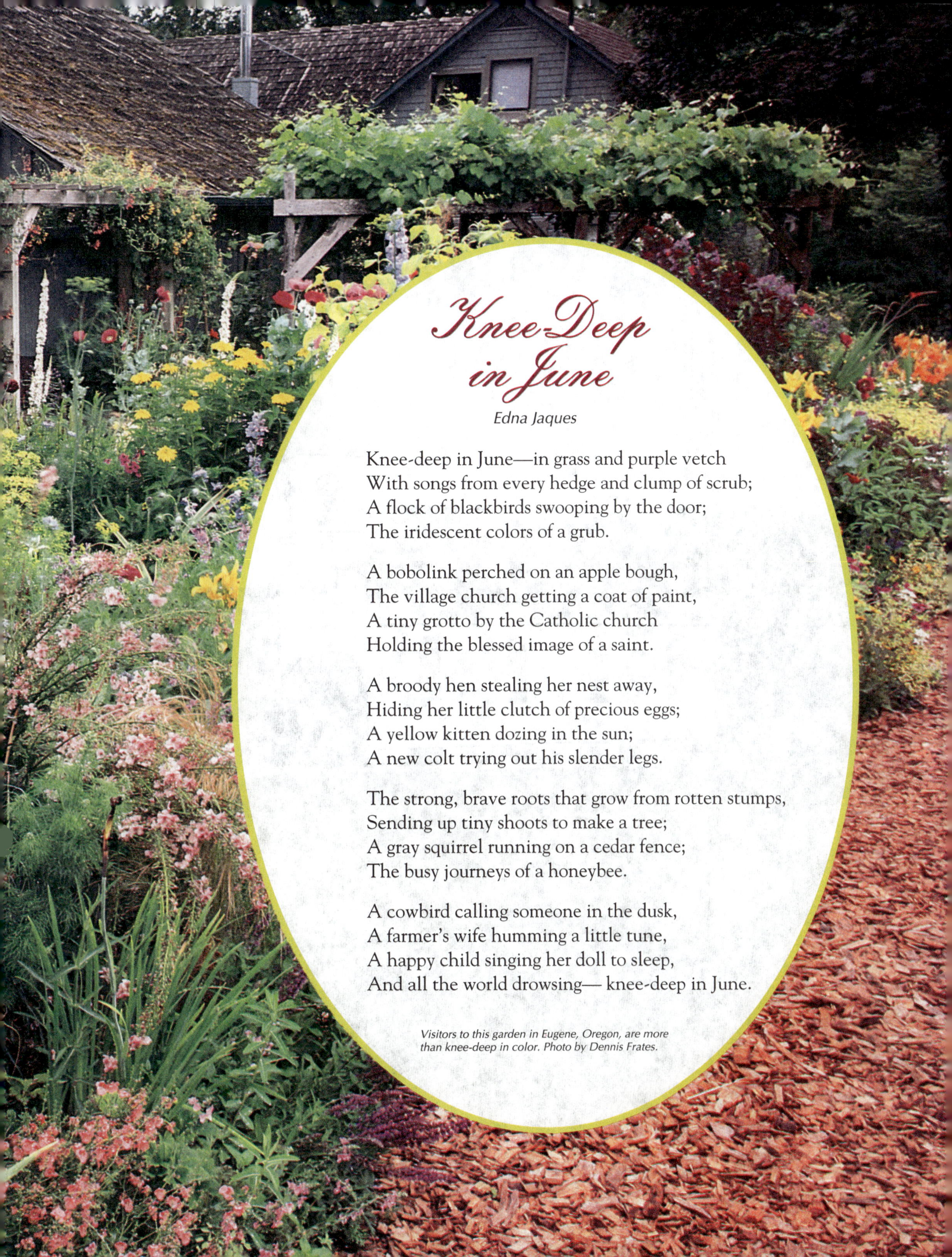

Knee-Deep in June

Edna Jaques

Knee-deep in June—in grass and purple vetch
With songs from every hedge and clump of scrub;
A flock of blackbirds swooping by the door;
The iridescent colors of a grub.

A bobolink perched on an apple bough,
The village church getting a coat of paint,
A tiny grotto by the Catholic church
Holding the blessed image of a saint.

A broody hen stealing her nest away,
Hiding her little clutch of precious eggs;
A yellow kitten dozing in the sun;
A new colt trying out his slender legs.

The strong, brave roots that grow from rotten stumps,
Sending up tiny shoots to make a tree;
A gray squirrel running on a cedar fence;
The busy journeys of a honeybee.

A cowbird calling someone in the dusk,
A farmer's wife humming a little tune,
A happy child singing her doll to sleep,
And all the world drowsing— knee-deep in June.

Visitors to this garden in Eugene, Oregon, are more than knee-deep in color. Photo by Dennis Frates.

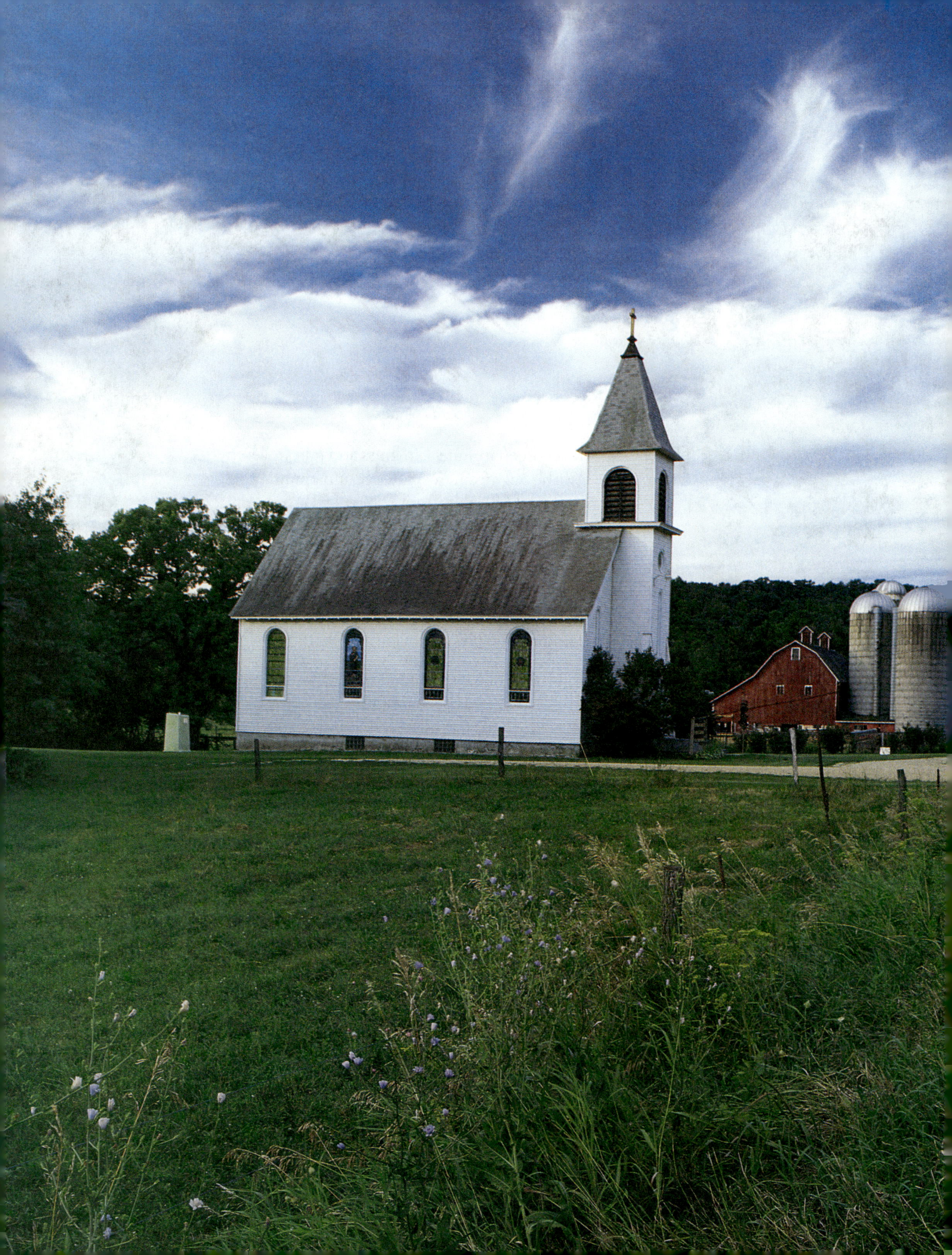

Where the Green Grass Grows

Alice Mills

I know where the green grass grows—
The greenest grass you'll ever know,
The softest blades beneath bare feet,
The sweetest smell in summer's heat.

I know where the blue sky spreads—
The bluest sky o'er any head,
The purest air from mountain springs,
The gentlest winds of insect wings.

I know where the green grass grows—
Underneath its owner's toes;
I know where the blue sky spreads,
Up above a free man's head.

I know where the red rose blooms—
The reddest rose of any June,
The smoothest velvet petal skin,
The rich incense of summers been.

I know where the gold sun shines—
The goldest sun of any clime,
The burnished beams for ripening grain,
The lulling warmth for children's games.

I know where the gold sun shines—
Only in a brave man's mind;
I know where the white dove sings—
In a land where church bells ring.

A church and barnyard share the same rural landscape in Iowa County, Wisconsin. Photo by Darryl Beers.

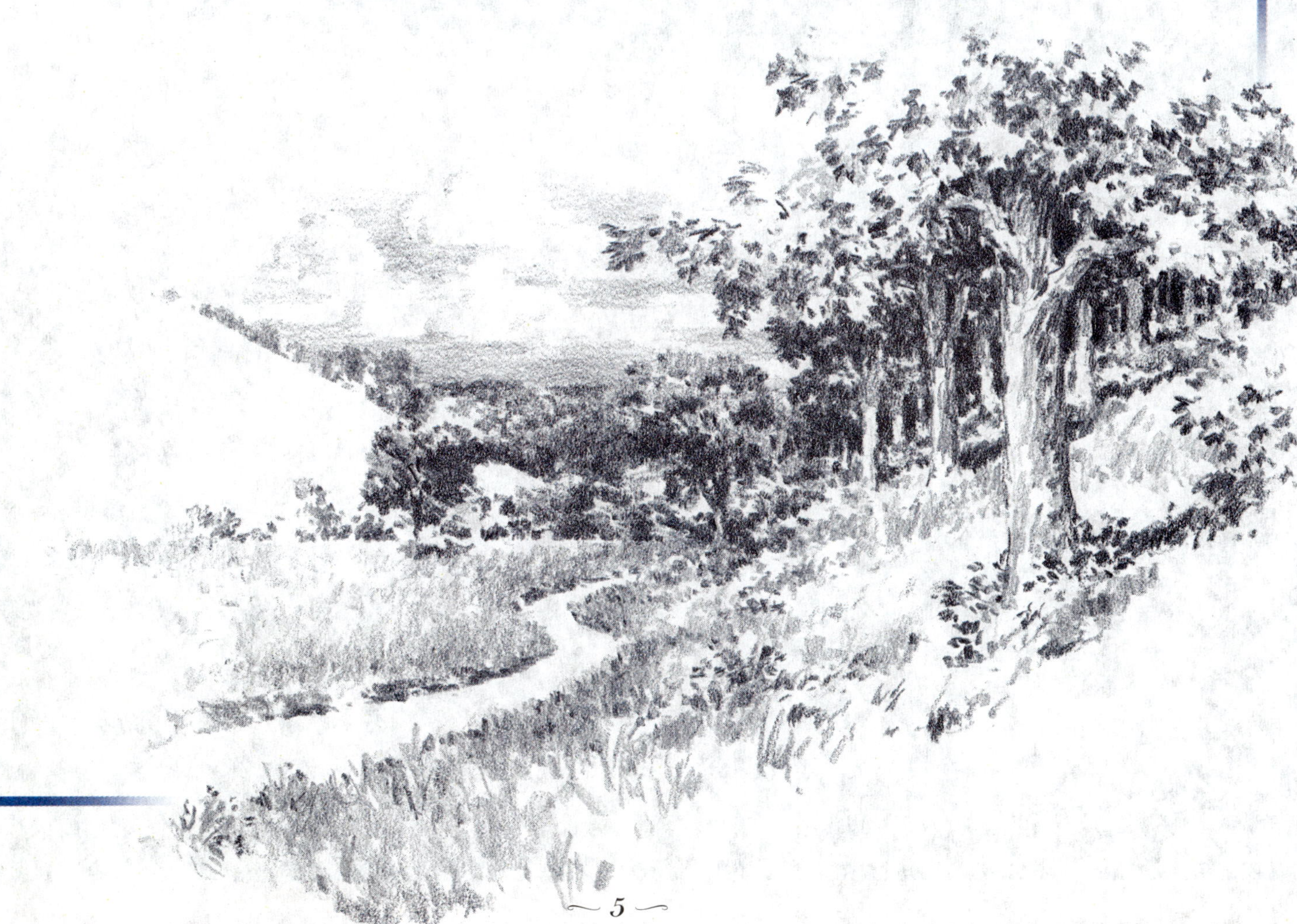

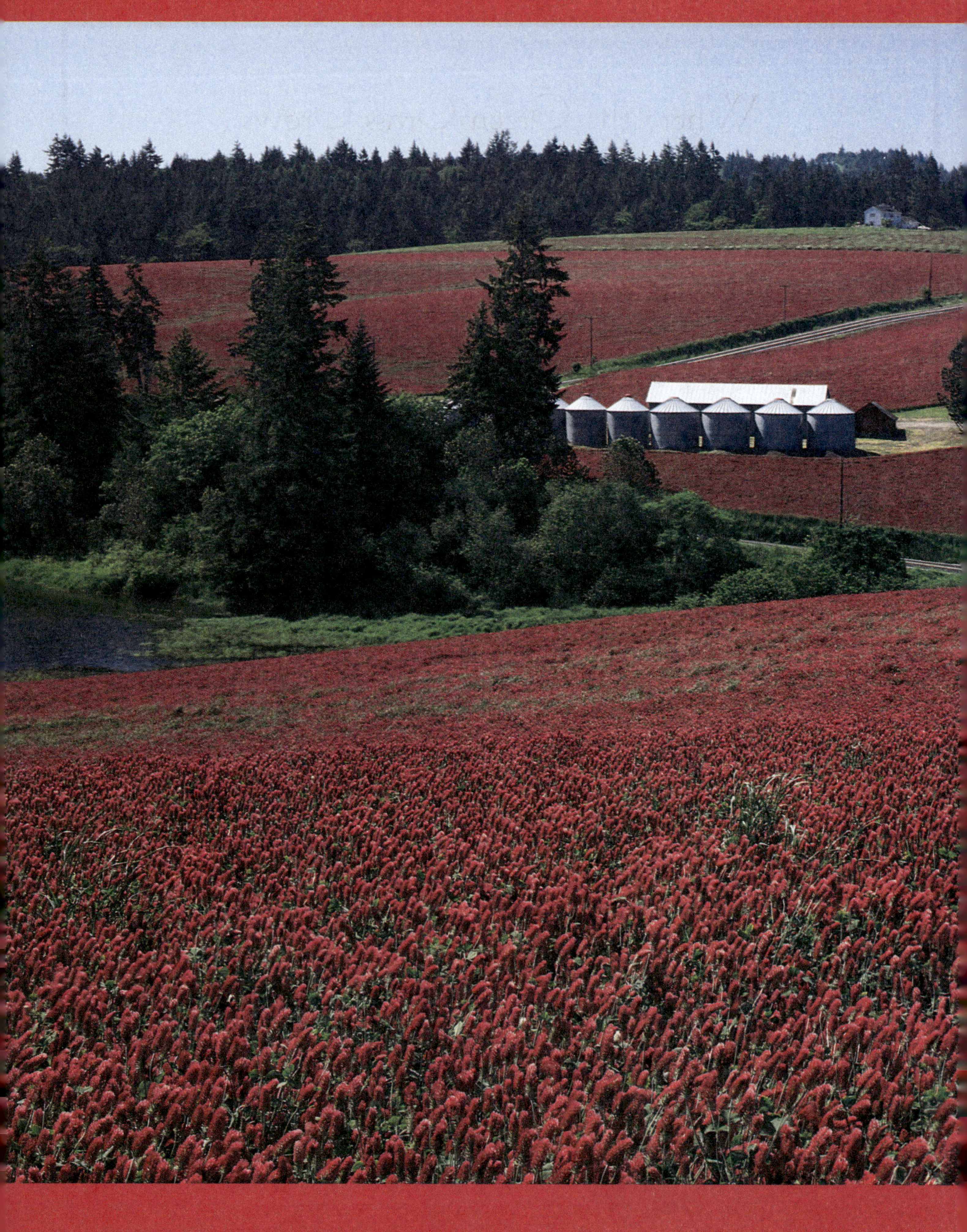

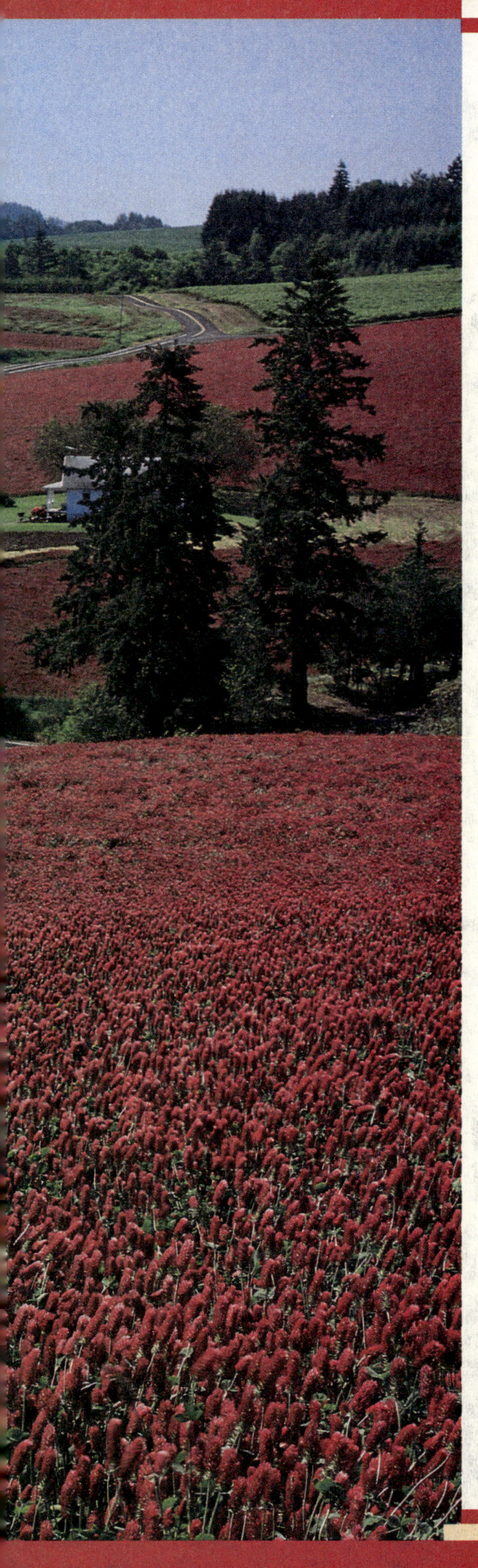

Clover

Helen Virden

In common things of earth we find the gold—
The peasantry of grass, the need for bread,
The streams of water running icy cold,
And fields of clover, growing white and red.

Its two-lipped flowers make a feast for bees.
Bright butterflies cling to its honeyed scent,
And creeping roots can harbor colonies
Of germs to nourish soil overspent.

Its growing leaves the world a better place;
For trooping down the dusty roadsides where
More haughty flowers refuse to show their face,
It leaves a trail of beauty like a prayer.
So generously it covers green the earth;
We sometimes fail to know its minted worth.

Crimson clover I discover
In the open field,
Mellow sunlight brooding over,
All her warmth revealed.

—**Dora Read Goodale**

This page: Clover creates nature's red carpet in the Chehalem Mountains of Oregon. Photo by Steve Terrill.
Overleaf: Each rock and flower points toward the summer sky in Colorado's White River National Forest. Photo by Carr Clifton.

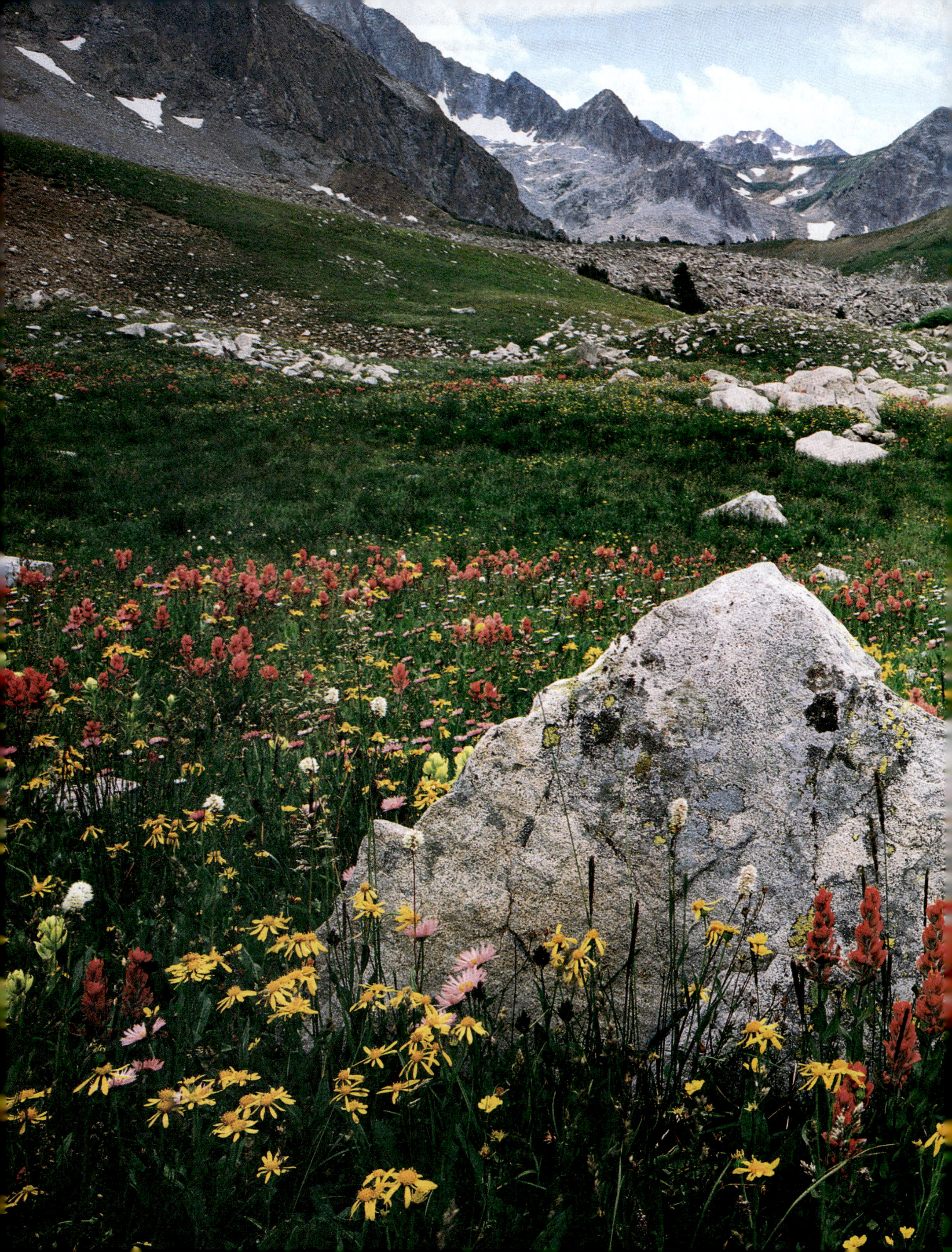

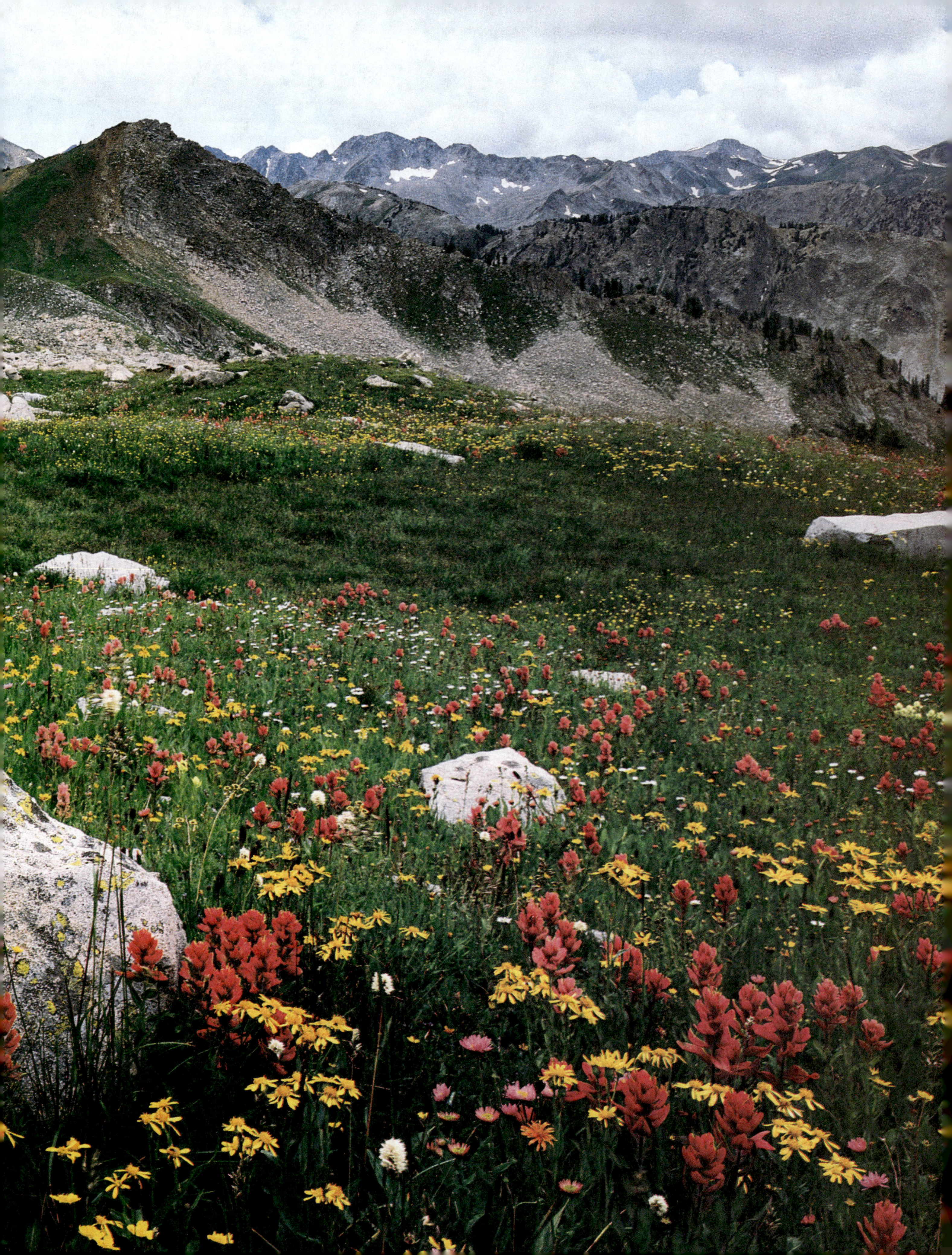

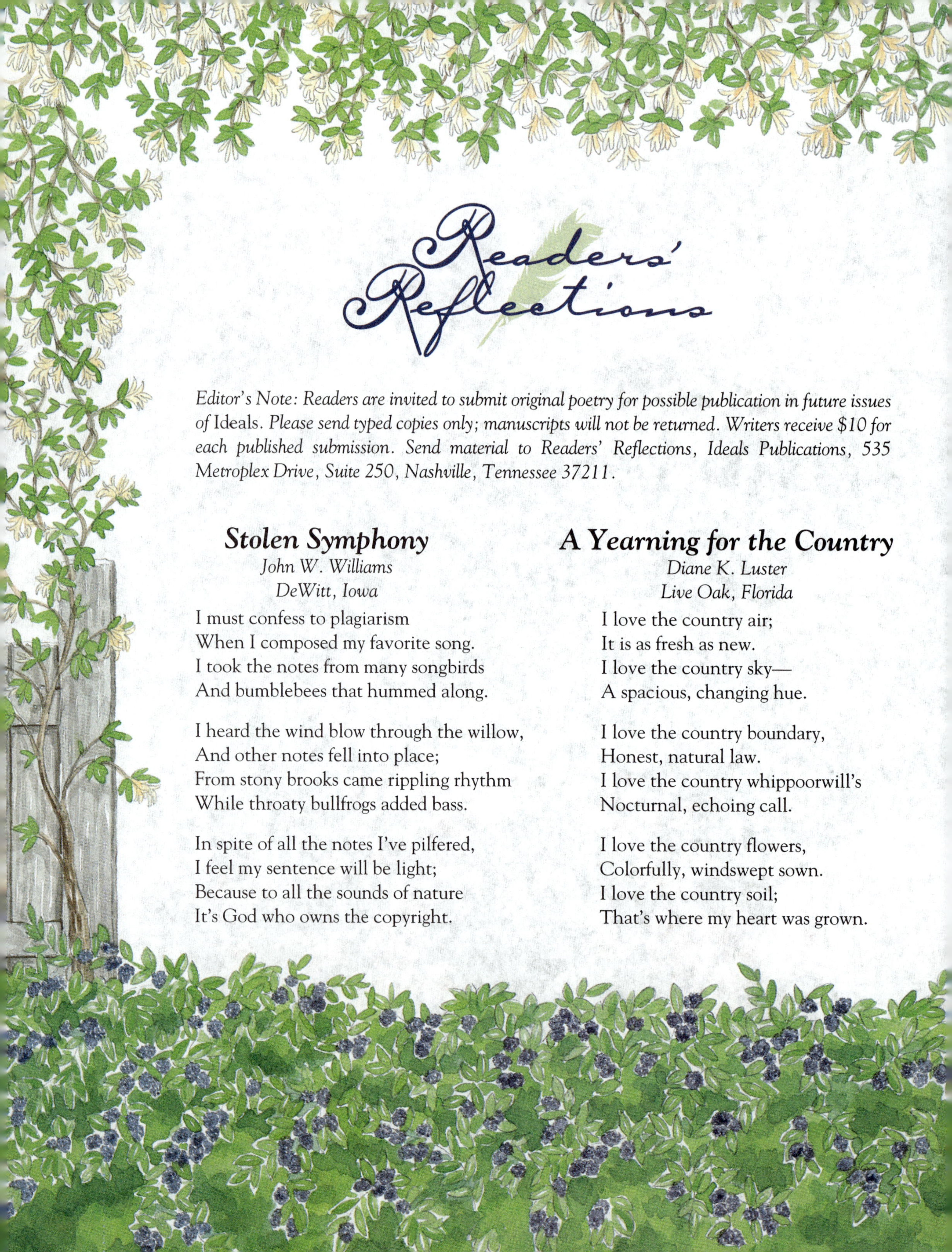

Readers' Reflections

Editor's Note: Readers are invited to submit original poetry for possible publication in future issues of Ideals. Please send typed copies only; manuscripts will not be returned. Writers receive $10 for each published submission. Send material to Readers' Reflections, Ideals Publications, 535 Metroplex Drive, Suite 250, Nashville, Tennessee 37211.

Stolen Symphony

John W. Williams
DeWitt, Iowa

I must confess to plagiarism
When I composed my favorite song.
I took the notes from many songbirds
And bumblebees that hummed along.

I heard the wind blow through the willow,
And other notes fell into place;
From stony brooks came rippling rhythm
While throaty bullfrogs added bass.

In spite of all the notes I've pilfered,
I feel my sentence will be light;
Because to all the sounds of nature
It's God who owns the copyright.

A Yearning for the Country

Diane K. Luster
Live Oak, Florida

I love the country air;
It is as fresh as new.
I love the country sky—
A spacious, changing hue.

I love the country boundary,
Honest, natural law.
I love the country whippoorwill's
Nocturnal, echoing call.

I love the country flowers,
Colorfully, windswept sown.
I love the country soil;
That's where my heart was grown.

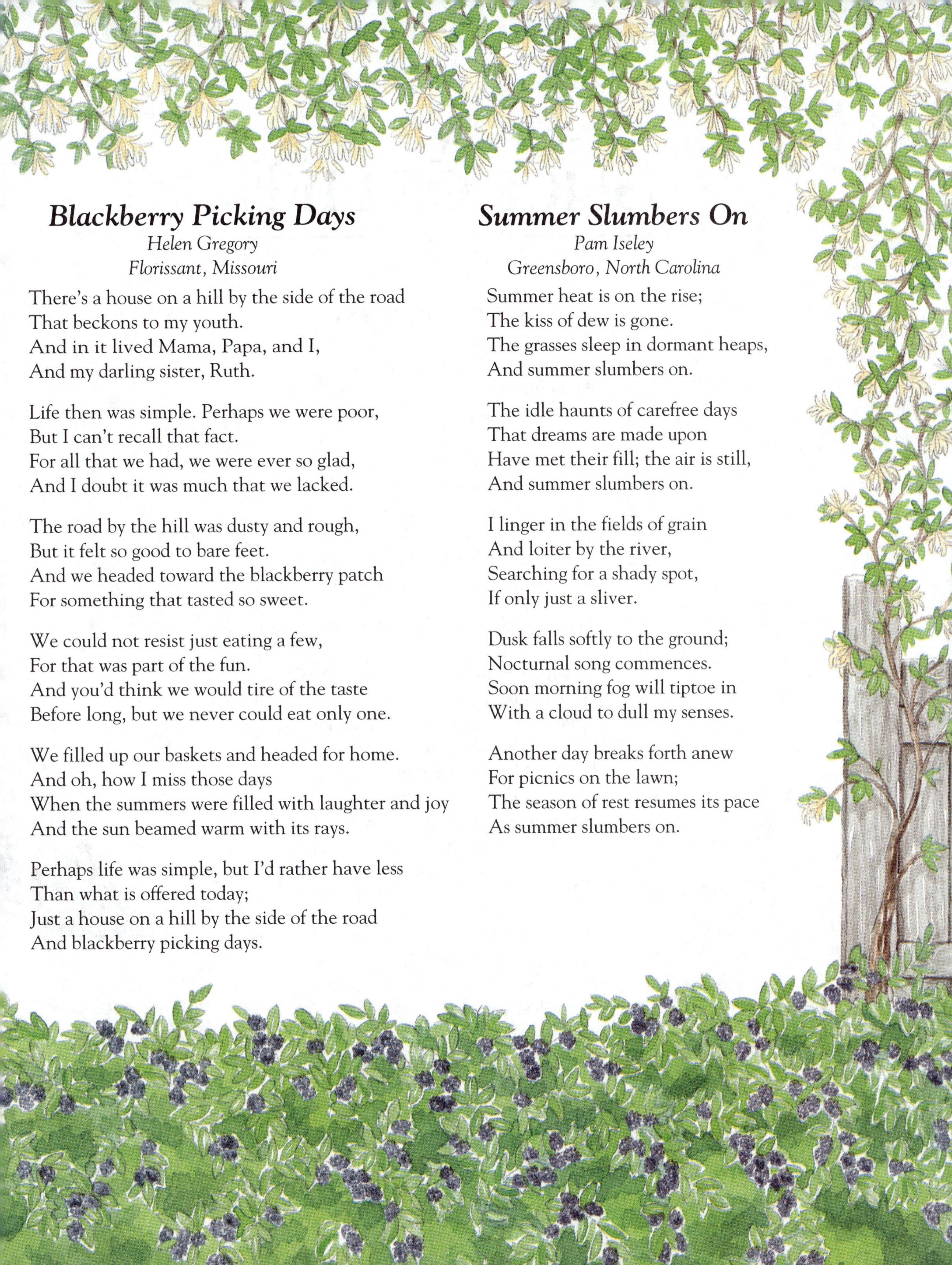

Blackberry Picking Days

Helen Gregory
Florissant, Missouri

There's a house on a hill by the side of the road
That beckons to my youth.
And in it lived Mama, Papa, and I,
And my darling sister, Ruth.

Life then was simple. Perhaps we were poor,
But I can't recall that fact.
For all that we had, we were ever so glad,
And I doubt it was much that we lacked.

The road by the hill was dusty and rough,
But it felt so good to bare feet.
And we headed toward the blackberry patch
For something that tasted so sweet.

We could not resist just eating a few,
For that was part of the fun.
And you'd think we would tire of the taste
Before long, but we never could eat only one.

We filled up our baskets and headed for home.
And oh, how I miss those days
When the summers were filled with laughter and joy
And the sun beamed warm with its rays.

Perhaps life was simple, but I'd rather have less
Than what is offered today;
Just a house on a hill by the side of the road
And blackberry picking days.

Summer Slumbers On

Pam Iseley
Greensboro, North Carolina

Summer heat is on the rise;
The kiss of dew is gone.
The grasses sleep in dormant heaps,
And summer slumbers on.

The idle haunts of carefree days
That dreams are made upon
Have met their fill; the air is still,
And summer slumbers on.

I linger in the fields of grain
And loiter by the river,
Searching for a shady spot,
If only just a sliver.

Dusk falls softly to the ground;
Nocturnal song commences.
Soon morning fog will tiptoe in
With a cloud to dull my senses.

Another day breaks forth anew
For picnics on the lawn;
The season of rest resumes its pace
As summer slumbers on.

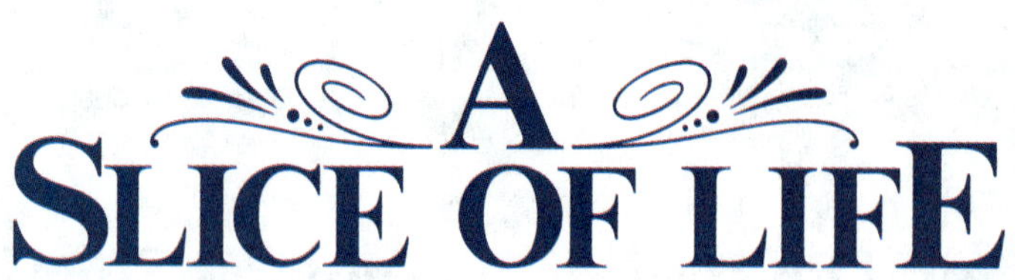

Douglas Malloch

Art by Eve DeGrie

The Boy on First

Forgive me, folks, if I am proud
And hold my head above the crowd
And act as if I'm satisfied
With me myself, the man inside.
It isn't that at all, at all;
But see that boy who caught the ball
And touched the bag and made an out?
Well, that's what I am proud about.
That's why I'm proud enough to burst,
For that's my youngster playing first.

There's pride and *pride*, and one's the kind
That ordinarily you find
When someone's proud of him himself:
His job, his title, or his pelf.
And yet the only pride worthwhile,
To give you joy and make you smile,
Is when it's someone that you love;
It's someone else you're proudest of—
A boy on first who bears your name
And loves his dad and plays the game.

A man must scrimp a hundred ways
To raise a family these days.
But he can work and he can win,
Work day and night and work like sin,
If he can have, to make him glad,
A boy he's proud of, lucky dad!
And boys, you boys, remember that—
That's what he's working for and at:
Just be the boy at school, at play,
Your dad is proud of every day.

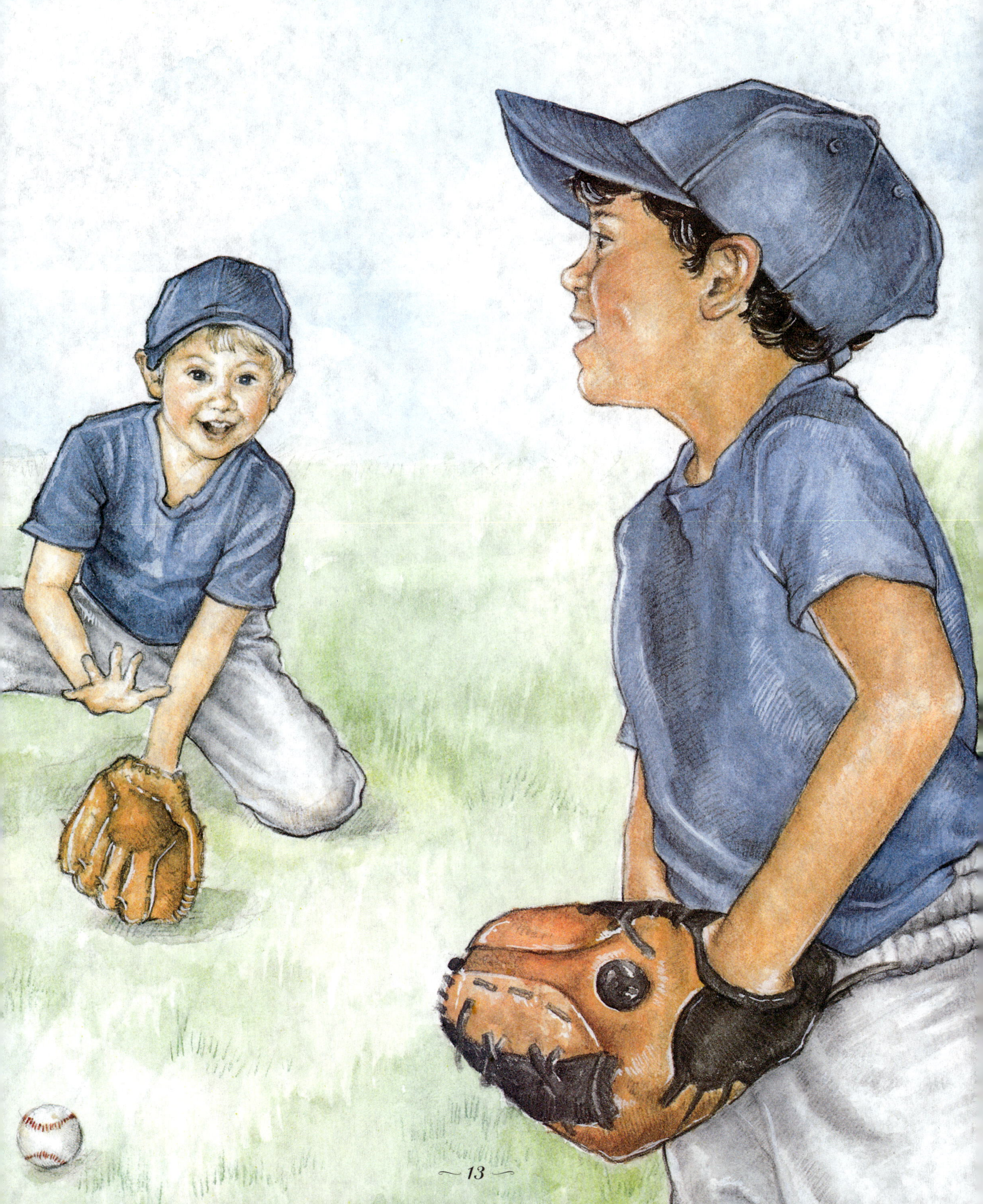

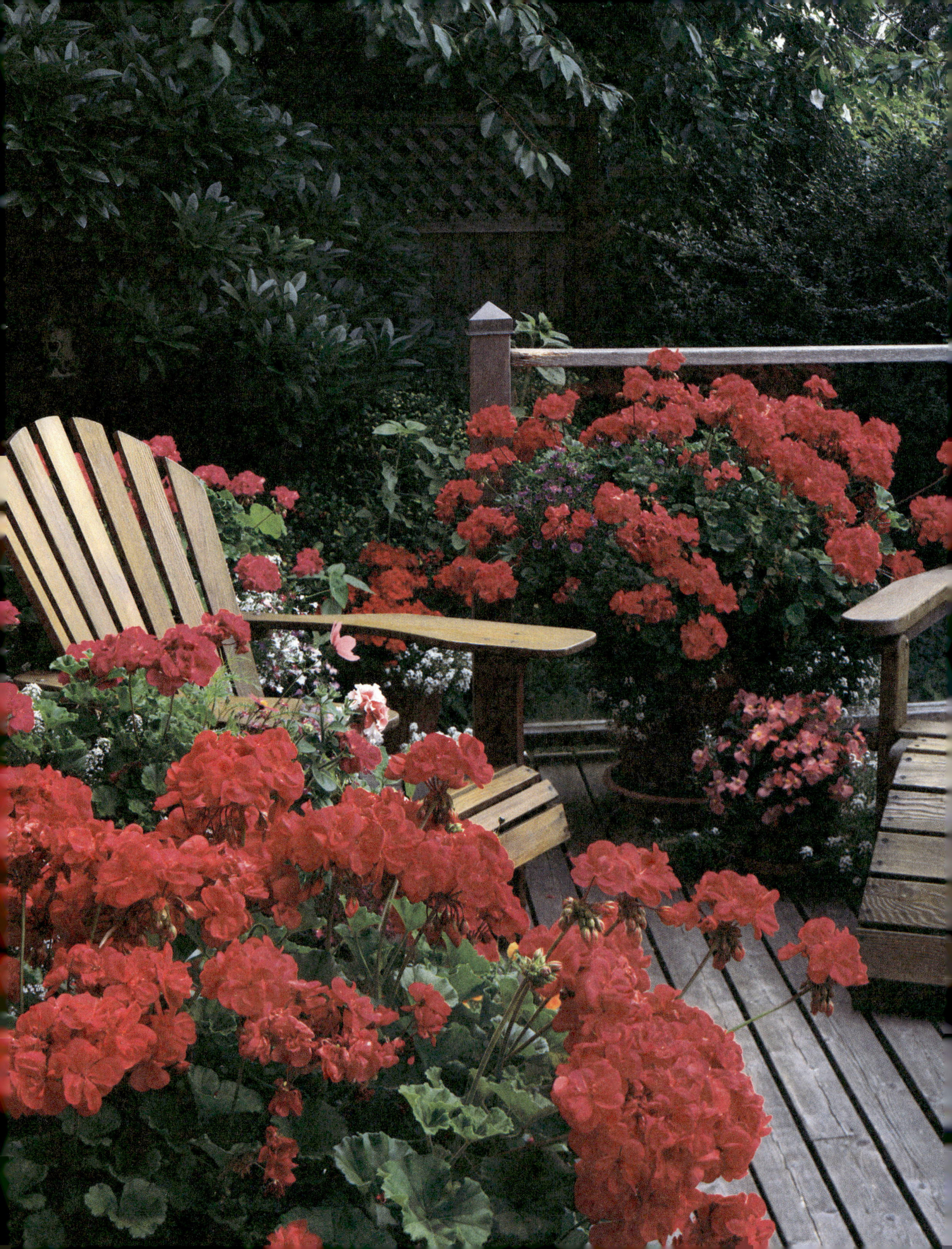

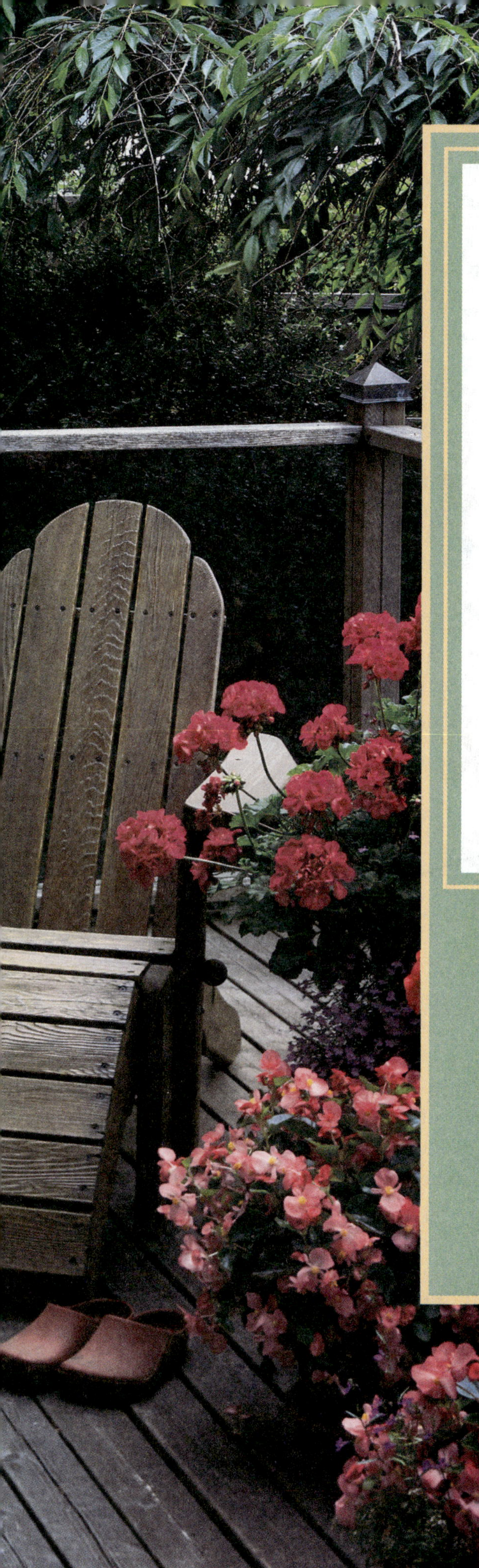

Peace

John Ruskin

To get peace, if you do want it, make for yourselves nests of pleasant thoughts. None of us yet knows, for none of us has been taught in early youth, what fairy palaces we may build of beautiful thoughts—proof against all adversity. Bright fancies, satisfied memories, noble histories, faithful sayings, treasure-houses of precious and restful thoughts: these are things which care cannot disturb, nor pain make gloomy, nor poverty take away from us—houses built without hands for our souls to live in.

A beautiful container garden creates a secluded nook in Vashon Island, Washington. Photo by Mary Liz Austin.

Oh, for a seat in some
secluded nook
Just hid with trees and
sparkling with a brook.

—LEIGH HUNT

THROUGH MY WINDOW

Pamela Kennedy

Art by Meredith Johnson

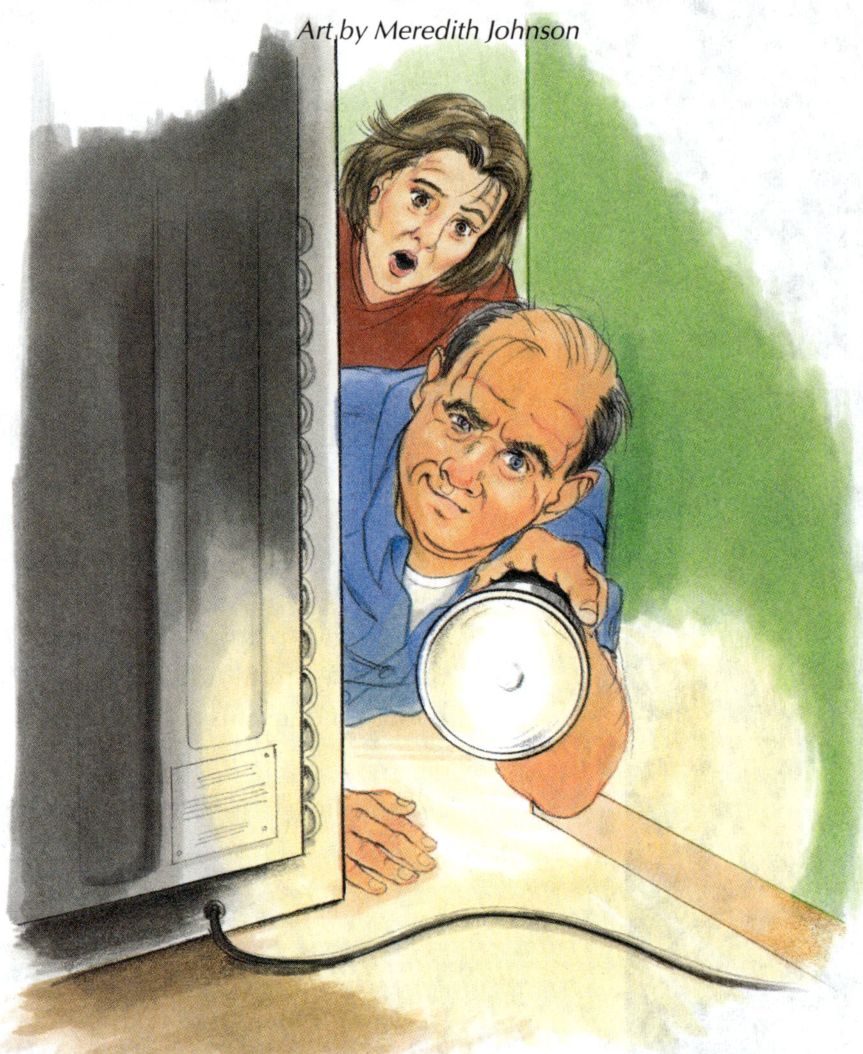

UNINVITED HOUSEGUESTS

It all started when we pulled out the refrigerator in order to check behind it for a lost recipe card. My husband shone the flashlight in the darkness behind the white behemoth and discovered, along with my lasagna recipe, an unusual bulge in the wall.

"Look at that," he said, sounding puzzled. I looked.

"What do you suppose is causing that?" I asked. We felt the bump and it was cool, dry, and solid. "Do you think something is leaking back there? But it doesn't feel wet." I answered my own question.

"I don't know, but I'll call someone to come and take a look. It's probably a leak."

A few days later, Mike from "Leak Busters" handed me his card at the front door and announced he had come to check things out. We hauled the refrigerator away from the wall, and Mike squeezed in behind it to do his detective work. He knocked on the wall and ran his hands over the bulge, which now looked much larger than it had a few days earlier. He said he didn't think it was a leak because it "knocked solid." I didn't say much, not being a certified leak buster myself.

Our house is built into a hillside, and the lower five feet of the inside kitchen wall is below ground. I was beginning to think we might have an alien of some sort lurking behind there. Could it be some weird underground creature, hiding, raising its young, waiting to make its escape some night when there was a full moon and the gestation cycle was completed? "What do you think it is?" I whispered to Mike.

"Don't know, but this baby will tell us," he said,

opening a brushed aluminum case and revealing a device that looked very similar to the thing the doctor used when I had a series of upper GI tests. "This is my secret weapon." It was becoming clear that Mike took his job very seriously. He reverently lifted the stainless steel pieces out of their foam-enclosed slots and fit them together until he had something resembling a periscope with a light. Then he punched a small hole in the wall and stuck the end of his instrument into it. Peering into the eyepiece, he was quiet for a few seconds, and then he let out a low whistle. "Wow, you don't see this too often. Want to take a look?" He moved back from the scope and allowed me to peer through it. What I saw confirmed my worst fears. There was an alien behind the wall!

The hole Mike had punched in the wall was roiling with small white bodies, hundreds or maybe thousands of them. When he pulled the scope out of the wall, they poured out onto the floor, and I stepped back in disgust. "Oh, yuck! What are they?" I wailed.

"Lady, you've got termites big time." Mike spoke with authority. As he snapped apart his scope and replaced it in its case, he explained that they had probably gotten through a crack in the foundation, eaten up the supports behind the wallboard, and allowed the dirt to press into the wall, forming the bulge. "No leak here," he announced. "Guess you'll have to call the exterminators." He filled the hole with a wad of paper towel, and I wondered how long that would keep out an invading army that had already eaten through lumber and wallboard.

The next day I called the exterminators, Jerry and Jeff. They showed up in a late-model van sporting a dead six-foot roach painted on the side. I guess if you're in pest control, you want to leave no doubt about the fate of your enemies. That was just fine with me.

After extracting the wad of paper towel, Jerry and Jeff agreed with Mike's diagnosis. They then explained to me how they were going to wrestle control of the wall back from the insect world. The plan was elegant. They would punch a couple more holes in the wall and place bait boxes filled with poisoned rolls of paper over the openings. The "workers" would eat the paper and carry the poison back to the queen, who was no doubt lurking fifty feet or more below the house in some terrestrial royal chamber. At this point they stopped and said, "Boy, you can make big bucks if you ever get the queen. The university will pay you lots of money—couple thousand dollars even!" I suggested that was sure a lot to pay for a little bug. That's when Jeff stood back with the assurance of one who knows much more about his field than the mere novice and said, "Lady, a termite queen is no little bug. They can be a foot to a foot-and-a-half long. Just one big termite-producing blob."

I really didn't need to know that. I shuddered and asked how long it would take for the workers to get their deadly lunch back to the queen.

"Oh, could be a couple of months, maybe less." Jerry and Jeff taped three of their traps up to the wall and pushed the fridge back. Then they left me with some paperwork and a promise to be back in a week to check on things. I stood there imagining the queen termite pumping out offspring who would chomp on my house and eat it up completely before Jerry and Jeff showed up in their dead roach van in seven days.

But the house remained standing. Over the course of the next few weeks, Jerry and Jeff and I became quite good friends. I baked them cookies, and they dutifully reported to me when the workers started to change to a creamy color (a bad thing if you're a termite), and when the soldiers started to show up (a sign that the queen isn't producing workers anymore), and when the soldiers stopped coming altogether (the very best sign of all). And when the dead roach van pulled out of the driveway for the last time, I felt a little sad that I wouldn't be seeing Jerry and Jeff anymore.

But I won't be too lonely, because I suspect that George the contractor and I will become good buddies as soon as he starts on the major repairs to the wall. And did I remember to tell you about my new friend Rhonda, at the insurance company, who had to break the news to me that our war against termites wasn't covered by our homeowner's policy because of the "vermin clause?" On the bright side, I've made all kinds of new acquaintances this year—all on account of my uninvited guests!

Pamela Kennedy is a freelance writer of short stories, articles, essays, and children's books. Wife of a retired naval officer and mother of three children, she has made her home on both U.S. coasts and currently resides in Honolulu, Hawaii.

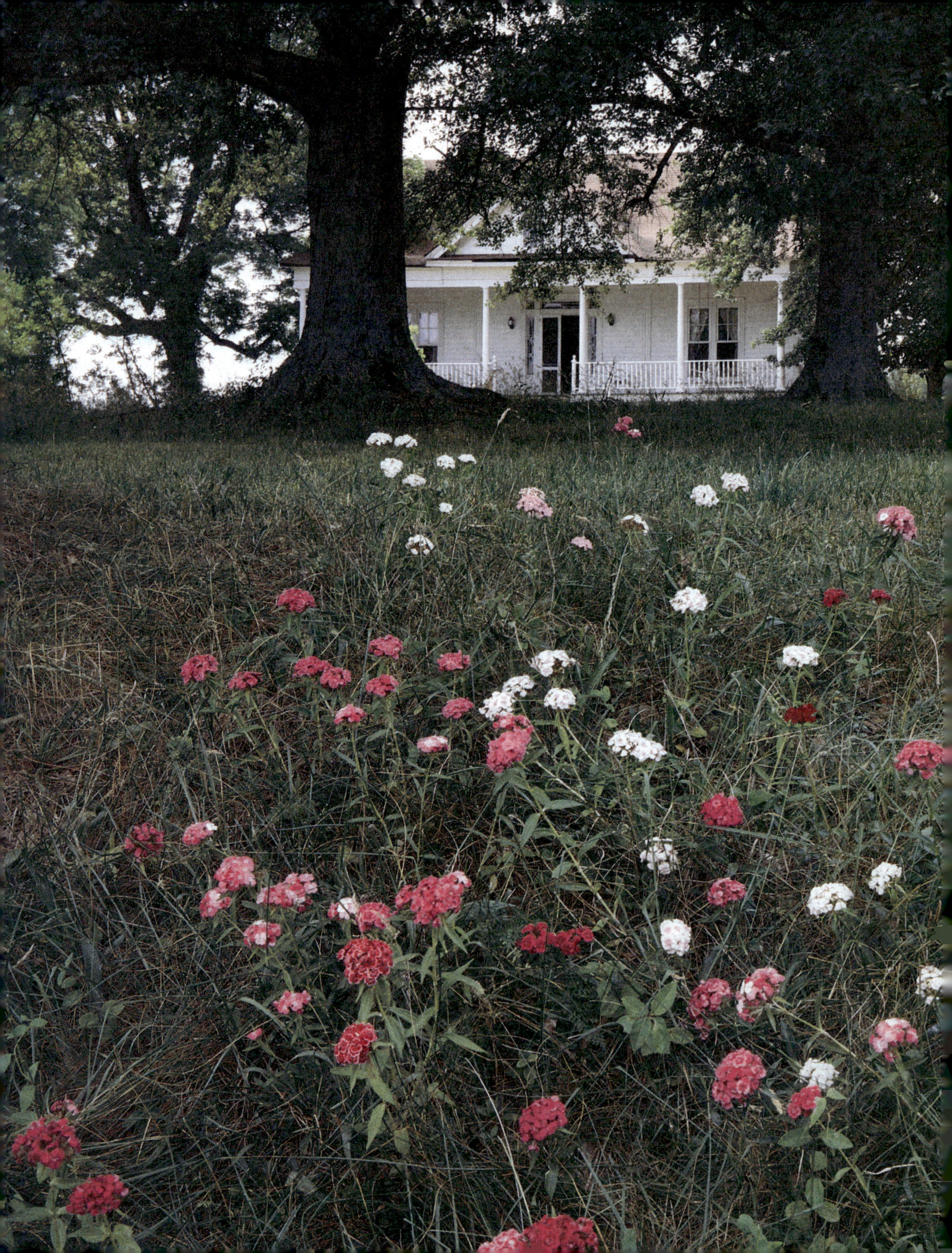

Who Lives There Now?

Mae Norton Morris

I wonder who lives where I used to live
In the little white house on the hill
Where wisteria twines o'er the low kitchen door
And shadows the scar-worn sill?

Do they love the glow of the evening lamp
When dusk creeps over the day
And find in the little room under the eaves
The harbor where dream ships lay?

Do they play 'neath the apple tree's gnarled old arms
And rest in its whispering shade
And loiter in spring by the garden's edge
To watch for each lily blade?

Who kneels for a breath of white violets now
And banks them when winds blow chill?
Oh, I wonder who lives where I used to live
In the little white house on the hill?

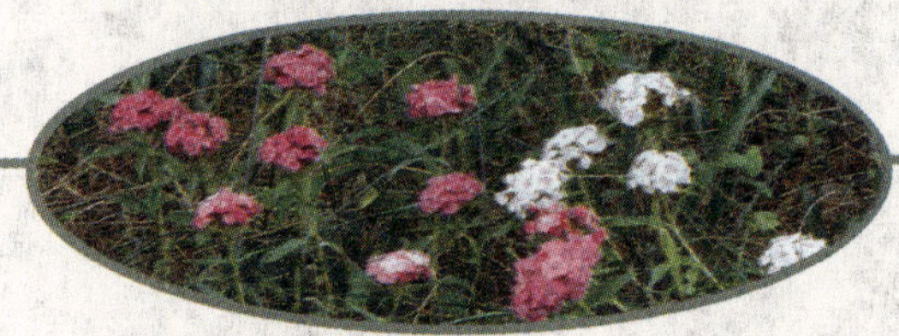

I Will Go Back a Little While

Nancy Byrd Turner

I will go back a little while and be
With old, untroubled things. There was a hill
Where huckleberries grew; there was a tree
No wind could harm. They both are standing, still.
There was that high, pure star I loved the best;
It still walks down the west.

No peril can befall them; they are part
Of everlasting loveliness and fold
Their peace around the far-returning heart.
I will go back and find them as of old
Then, fearless, face whatever storms may come,
Having been home.

Sweet William dots the yard of a long-standing home near Williamston, South Carolina. Photo by Norman Poole.

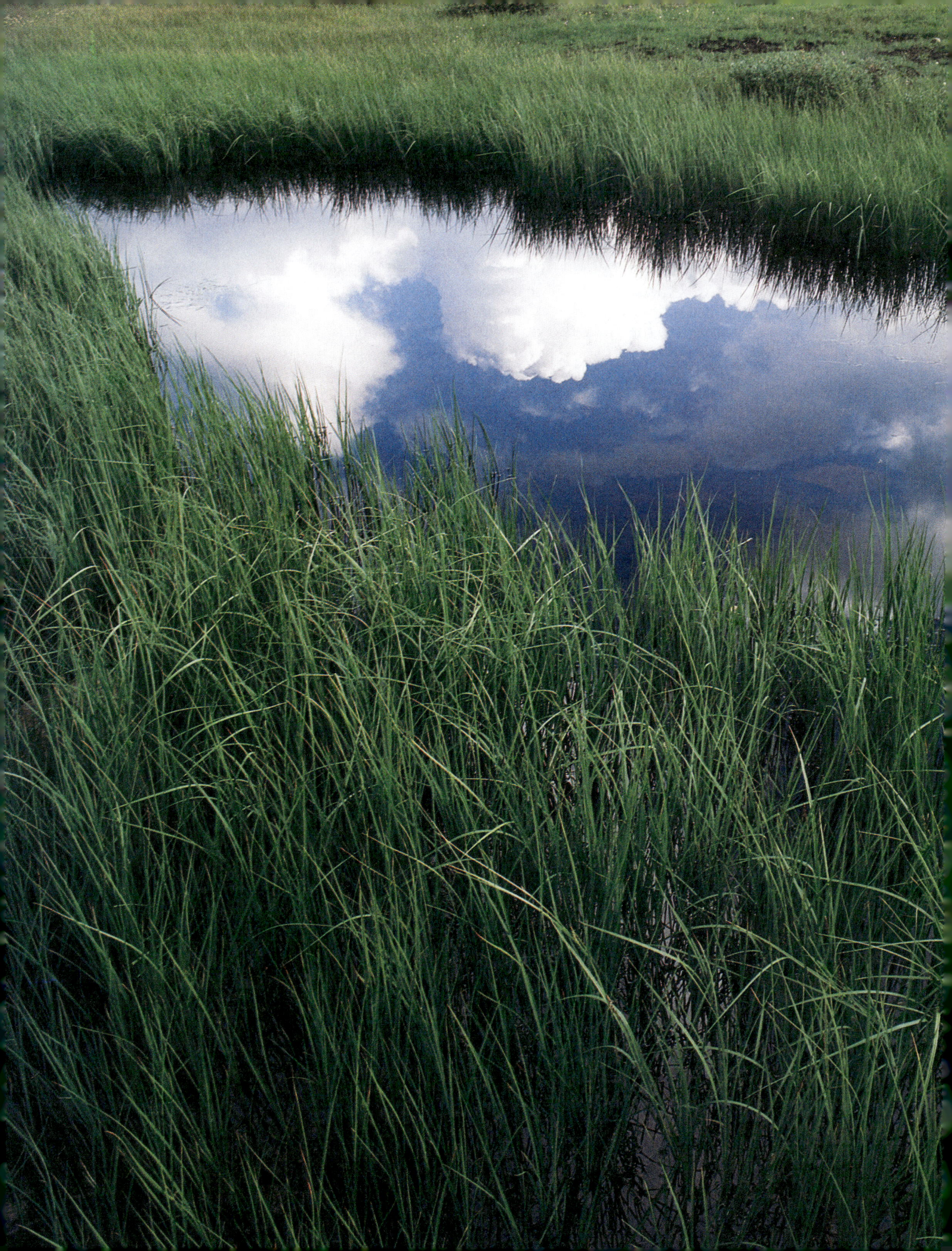

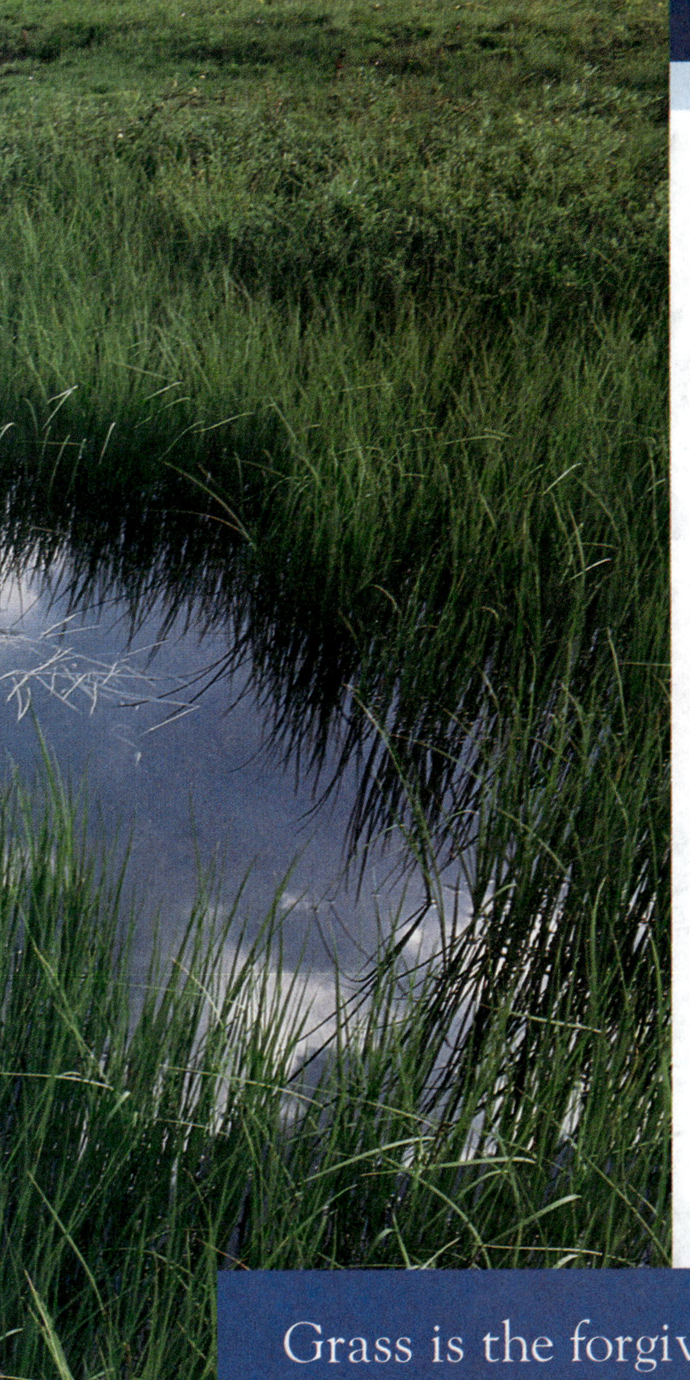

Grass

Lorice Fiani Mulhern

I love grass, long and waving—
Its warm, green fragrance,
Its silken sheen in the sun
all captivating.

I love its slender blades,
So strong and impervious—
Springing up sprightly, undaunted,
No matter how windswept or trodden.

I love grass close to rocks and flowers,
Spreading itself like a cloak for blossoms—
Or stretching for miles
And countless miles
Over rolling hills and meadows
As the earth's loveliest raiment.

I love grass, rainswept and dew laden,
Bearing gifts of newness and diamonds.

Grass is the forgiveness of nature—
her constant benediction.
Forests decay, harvests perish,
flowers vanish, but grass is immortal.
—John James Ingalls

A hidden pool reflects the clouds in California's Yosemite National Park. Photo by Londie G. Padelsky.

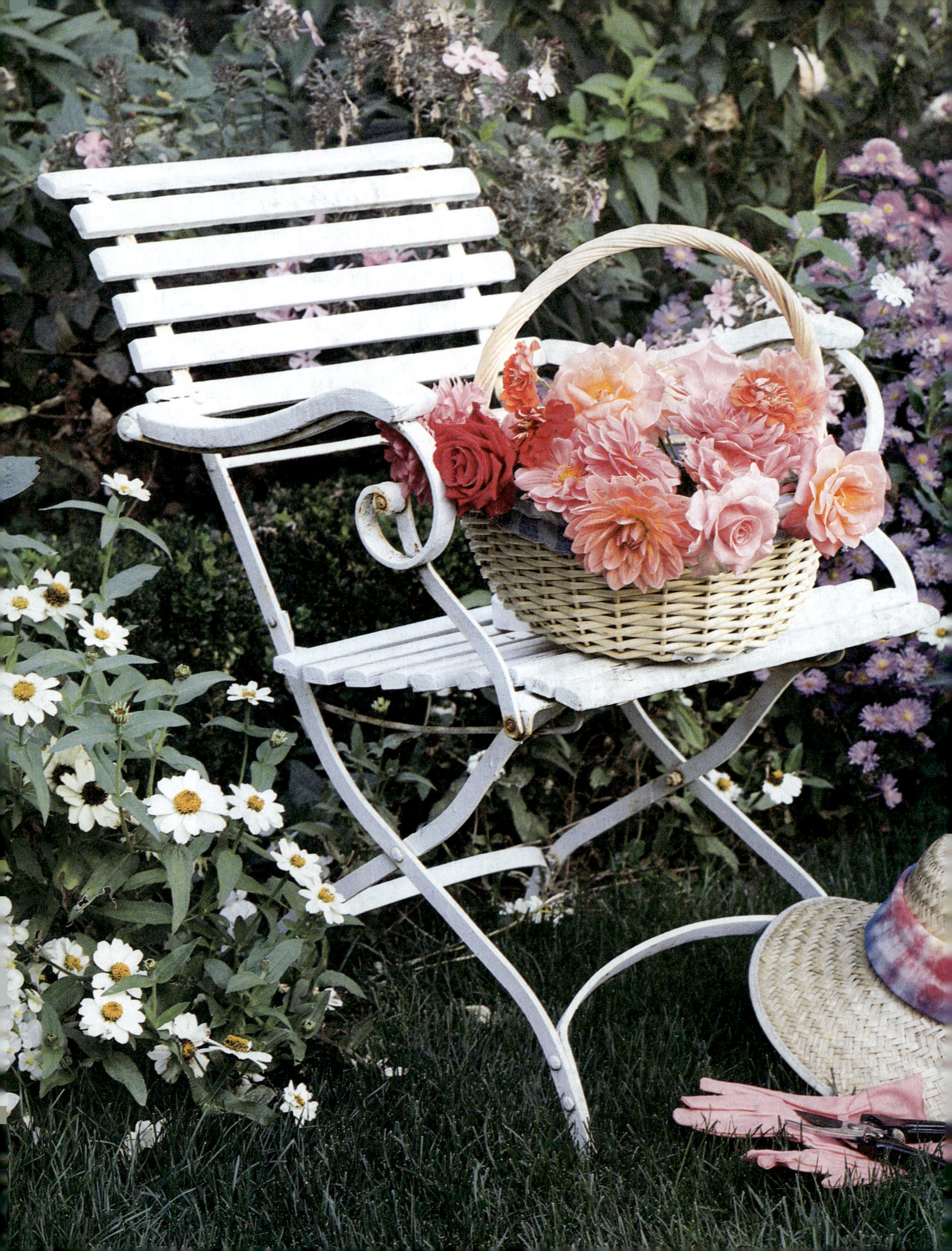

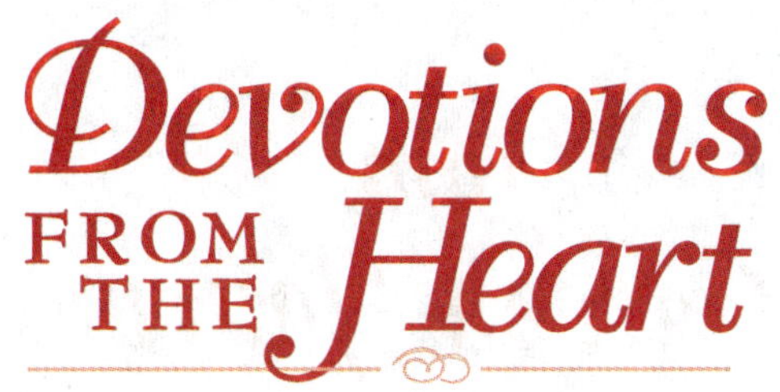

Pamela Kennedy

To every thing there is a season, and a time to every purpose under the heaven: A time to be born, and a time to die; a time to plant, and a time to pluck up that which is planted. Ecclesiastes 3:1–2

A Time to Grow

The end of the school year was approaching; and at the girls' school where I teach, the seniors were getting more excited by the day. College acceptances had been received; prom had come and gone. Baccalaureate would be in one week, then finals, and then graduation! Clusters of girls met to discuss plans for the big day. It was increasingly difficult for them to concentrate on their studies, and "senioritis" was spreading like wildfire. I tried to remember my own graduation day so many years ago, but all I could recall was a scene of nervous graduates marching solemnly into the gym in alternate rows of blue and white caps and gowns. I remember thinking that this was the beginning of my whole life. I guess in a way it was; but looking back at that hot June day now, I realize it was only the first in a long series of graduations.

In a sense, we are constantly graduating from one season of life to the next. As Solomon described in Ecclesiastes thousands of years ago, there is a time for every season under heaven. If we are actively growing, we continually experience these changing seasons to which Solomon referred.

Some of these seasonal changes are cause for celebration; but as Solomon reminds us, not all seasons are filled with joy. Births, or "plantings," are often filled with anticipation and excitement. We look forward to the future as we eagerly await what lies beyond and anticipate the additional blessings of new experiences. But there are also times of death, or "plucking up" that which is planted. We do not welcome these changes; and we may look ahead with fear, unsure of how we will manage, unsteady in a world that has changed and suddenly seems out of balance. Yet Solomon reminds us that if we view life from God's perspective, we will recognize that each season has its own purpose. We learn the lessons of a painful time, and we graduate to the position of compassion toward others. Our life takes us through a particularly wonderful stage, and we learn that we have the resources to encourage others financially or emotionally. Even uneventful times may give us the perspective we need to help others endure when their lives seem empty or pointless.

> Dear heavenly Father, please help me to embrace all the seasons of my life, so that I may never cease growing but continually enjoy Your good harvest of joy, peace, and faith.

When we resent the changing seasons of our lives, we lose opportunities for growth and increased faith. It is in the difficult times that God's still, small voice whispers, "I will never leave you nor forsake you." When we are coping with new challenges, Paul reminds us that we "can do all things through Christ who is [our] strength." Each seasonal change is a time of growth, of strengthening the muscles of trust, hope, and faith.

And the wisdom of Solomon also reminds us that even difficult times will give way to times of laughter, peace, and love. Life moves on, and so must we. Let us never forget that God ordains all the seasons of our lives, and He knows far better than we the areas in which we need to grow.

A basket of blooms waits to be arranged. Photo by Dianne Dietrich Leis/Dietrich Photography.

From My Garden Journal

Lisa Ragan

CORNFLOWER

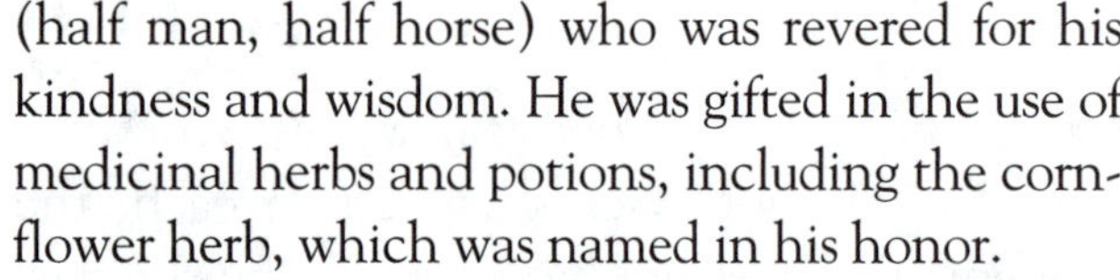

Blue thou art, intensely blue!
Flower! whence came thy dazzling hue?
When I opened first mine eye,
Upward glancing at the sky,
Straightway from the firmament
Was the sapphire brilliance sent.

These lines from British poet James Montgomery bring to my mind the vivid blue blossoms of the humble cornflower, although I doubt if his inspiration for this ode came from what for centuries was called the scourge of southern European farmers. Native to the Mediterranean and naturalized throughout most of Europe, the cornflower once grew profusely in cornfields, hence its common name. Farmers detested the unpopular weed and even dubbed it "hurtsickle" because of the way in which it dulled their sickles at reaping time.

The actual genus name for cornflower, *Centaurea cyanus*, has its own interesting lore. In Greek mythology, Chiron was a centaur (half man, half horse) who was revered for his kindness and wisdom. He was gifted in the use of medicinal herbs and potions, including the cornflower herb, which was named in his honor.

Despite the cornflower's decidedly unpopular status with European farmers, the flower made its way into English cottage gardens sometime during the Tudor era of the fifteenth, sixteenth, and seventeenth centuries. English gardeners delighted in the striking blue blossoms of this hardy annual, which they called a bluebottle or a bluet. Scottish gardeners referred to the cornflower as a bluebonnet, not to be confused with the bluebonnet celebrated throughout Texas.

A plant of many names, the cornflower traveled to the New World with the first colonists, who dubbed the flower ragged robin and ragged sailor as well as cornflower. By the Victorian era, gentlemen sported blue cornflower blossoms and called them bachelor's buttons. In fact, bachelor's buttons can now be found under the same genus name, *Centaurea cyanus*, as cornflower.

With improved grain harvesting, field clearing techniques, and the increased use of chemical weed killers, cornflowers rarely plague grain farmers today. The cornflower has, instead, become a cultivated garden bloomer with the old-fashioned look of a cottage garden flower.

Most cornflower plants feature gray-green foliage, but tiny white hairs cover their leaves and give them a blue-gray look. Each plant branches into many slender stems that produce an abundance of vibrantly colored blossoms one to two inches in diameter. Cornflower blossoms are inherently bright blue but can also be found

CORNFLOWER

in red, purple, maroon, pink, and white, as well as bicolored variations.

Dwarf cornflower plants can be grown without staking, but the taller varieties may need some support as they stretch to their full height, usually around three feet. A related but slightly different plant, the perennial cornflower (*Centaurea montana*), hails from the mountains of central Europe and will grow to one-and-a-half-feet high. Two dwarf varieties in the blue color are Blue Midget and Jubilee Gem, and two of the tall varieties in blue are Blue Boy and Emperor William. For color variations, gardeners can choose from Red Boy (red), Garnet (burgundy), Black Ball (dark maroon), and Snowman (white). Cornflowers can even be grown in bicolored pastel shades (frosty mixed).

The annual cornflower has proven itself such a hardy plant that it is often treated as a biannual and planted twice a year in some climates. For blooms from early summer to early fall, cornflower seeds can be sown in spring after the last frost. For blooms in early spring, seeds can be sown in warmer climates about a month before the first autumn frost. Gardeners in colder climates with plenty of snowfall can also sow cornflower seeds in fall for early spring blooms because the snow will blanket the tender seedlings and protect them from the bitter cold. Seeds usually germinate in about one to three weeks. Some gardeners try to start cornflower seeds indoors about four weeks before the last frost and then transplant the seedlings to the flower bed, but these plants have not been known to take kindly to transplanting.

Seeds should be sown a quarter-inch deep and between eight and fourteen inches apart in a sunny location, although the plants will tolerate partial shade. Cornflower plants look particularly striking planted along roadsides, in meadows, or massed together as border plants. Gardeners have learned that this plant grows best if left unfertilized. If planted in poor soil, cornflower plants will bloom again and again with little care. If planted in rich soil, however, cornflower plants will produce glorious foliage and very few blossoms. When the plants reach about eight inches high, one can nip off about an inch of growth to inspire more branching and thus more flowers. These drought-tolerant annuals need occasional removal of dead flower heads to curb their self-sowing habit and to encourage more blooms.

Gardeners should watch their cornflower plants for aphid infestations, which can bring down entire plants if left unchecked. Cornflowers do their part to keep the garden healthy, however. Nectar slowly seeps from the cornflower's leaves even when the plant is not in bloom. This nectar attracts such friendly insects as ladybugs, lacewings, hover flies, and beneficial wasps.

Cornflower blossoms have proven themselves to be long-lasting, vibrant cut flowers and make a great addition to a cutting garden. The vivid blooms also work well in flower arrangements; in fact, florists often select the blue cornflower for the blue in patriotic bouquets at Independence Day celebrations. The cornflower remains a popular choice as a dried flower also, because it retains much of its bright hue even when dried. When harvesting the cornflower blossom for drying, cut the flowers just as the blooms begin to open and hang them upside down in a cool, dry place for two weeks.

Even though James Montgomery may not have been writing lines of verse to the simple cornflower, this hardy bloomer is still praiseworthy. The cornflower faithfully produces celestial blue blossoms that are indeed of a most "dazzling hue." And where else but from the heavens above could such a brilliant color have come?

Lisa Ragan tends her small but mighty city garden in Nashville, Tennessee, with the help of her two shih-tzu puppies, Clover and Curry.

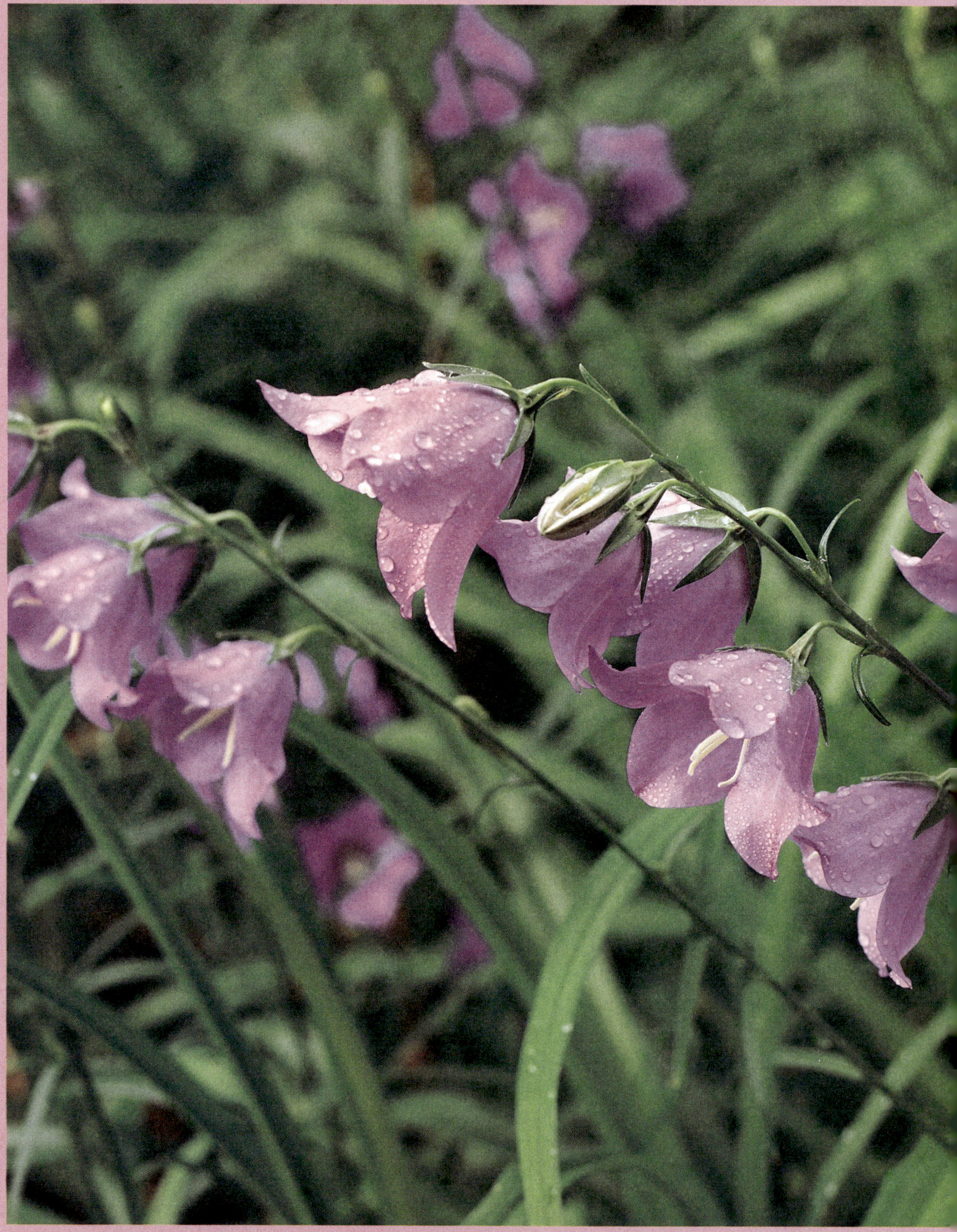

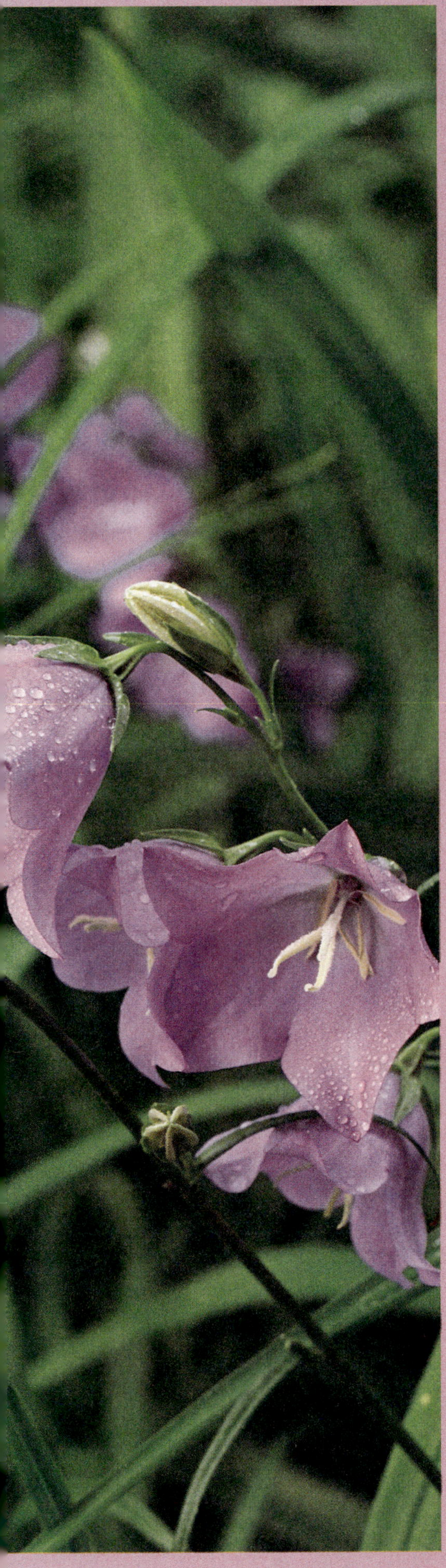

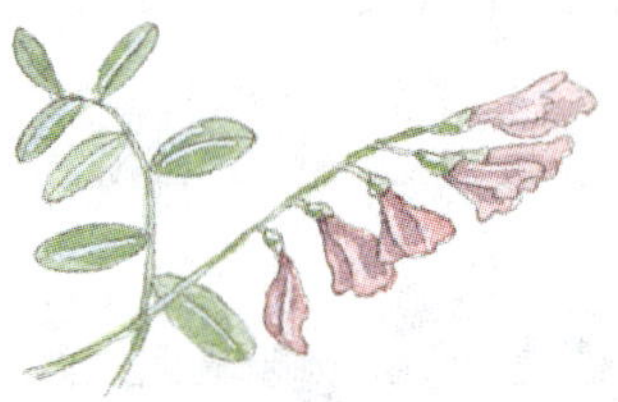

Rain in Summer

William Braithwaite

The afternoon grew darkening from the west;
A hush fell on the air and in the trees;
The huddled birds pronounced their prophecies.
The flowers bent their heads as if to rest
Now that the tide of the sun's golden seas
In one long wave swept off the earth's wide breast.
Up sprung deft shadowy patterns by degrees,
And nature's face her soul made manifest.
Lo, in the instant, slant, like a hanging string
Of silver glass beads, pendant from the clouds
The rain descends! Leaves sing, and wavering,
The tall lithe grasses dance in separate crowds.
I stand and let my soul commune; it knows
The mystery that calls it from its close.

Nature, like man,
sometimes weeps for gladness.

—BENJAMIN DISRAELI

Raindrops cling gently to harebells in Rockport, Maine.
Photo by William H. Johnson.

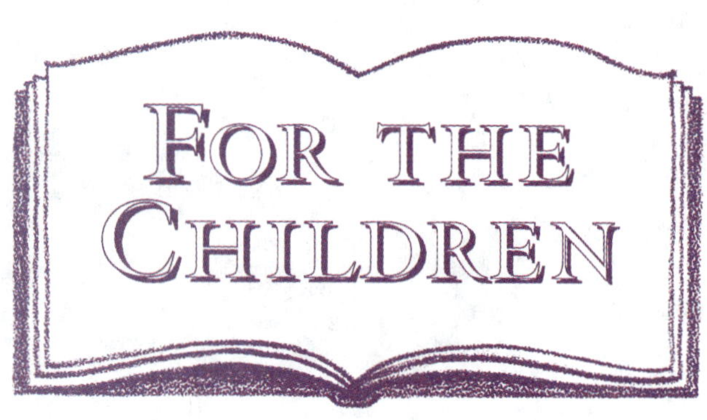

SEA SHELL

Amy Lowell

Sea shell, sea shell,
Sing me a song, O please!

A song of ships and sailormen
And parrots and tropical trees,
Of islands lost in the Spanish Main
Which no man ever may find again,
Of fishes and corals under the waves
And sea horses stabled in great green caves.

Sea shell, sea shell,
Sing of the things you know so well.

A young beachgoer listens for the ocean's music in SOUNDS OF THE SEA, *an original oil painting by artist Donald Zolan.*

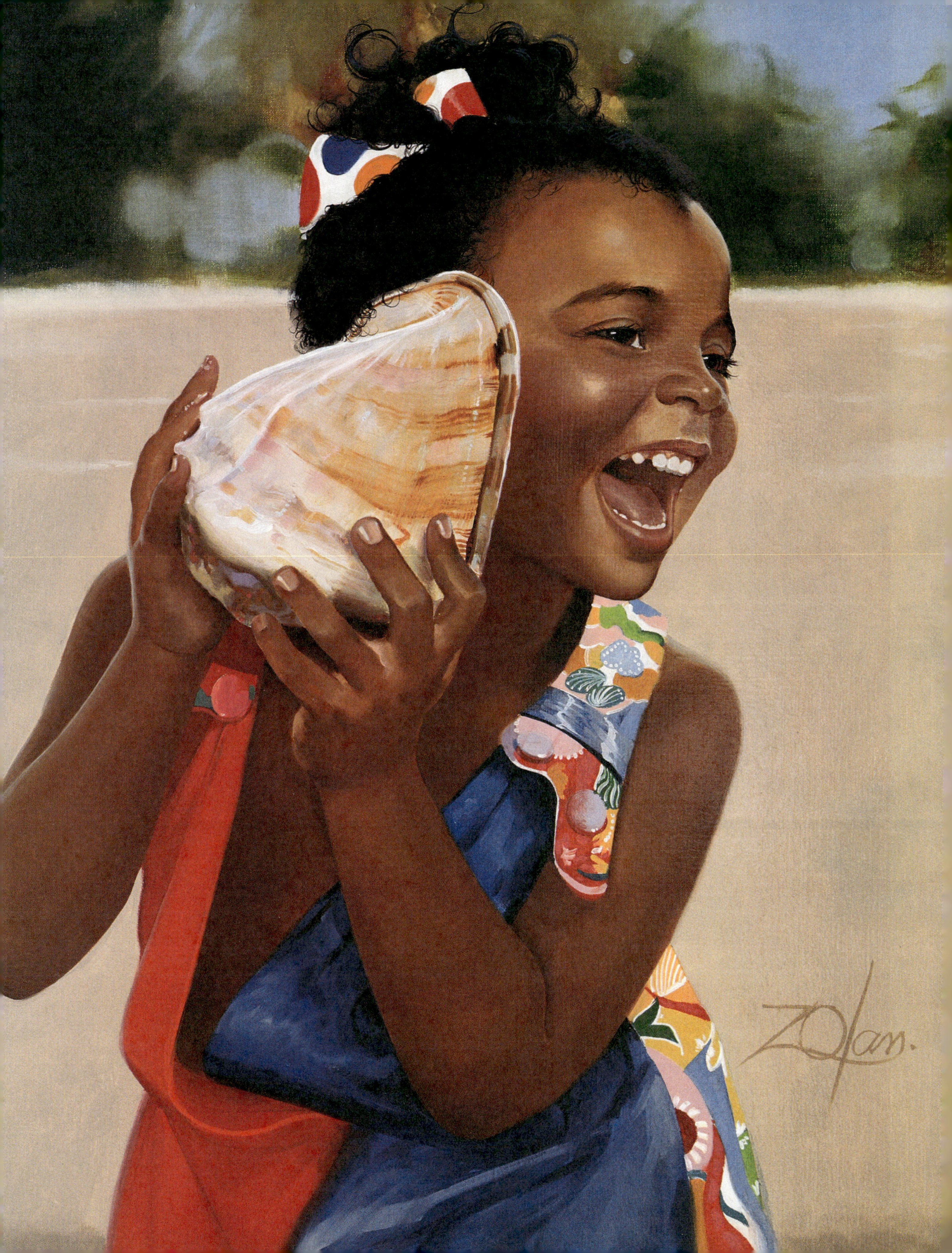
Zolan.

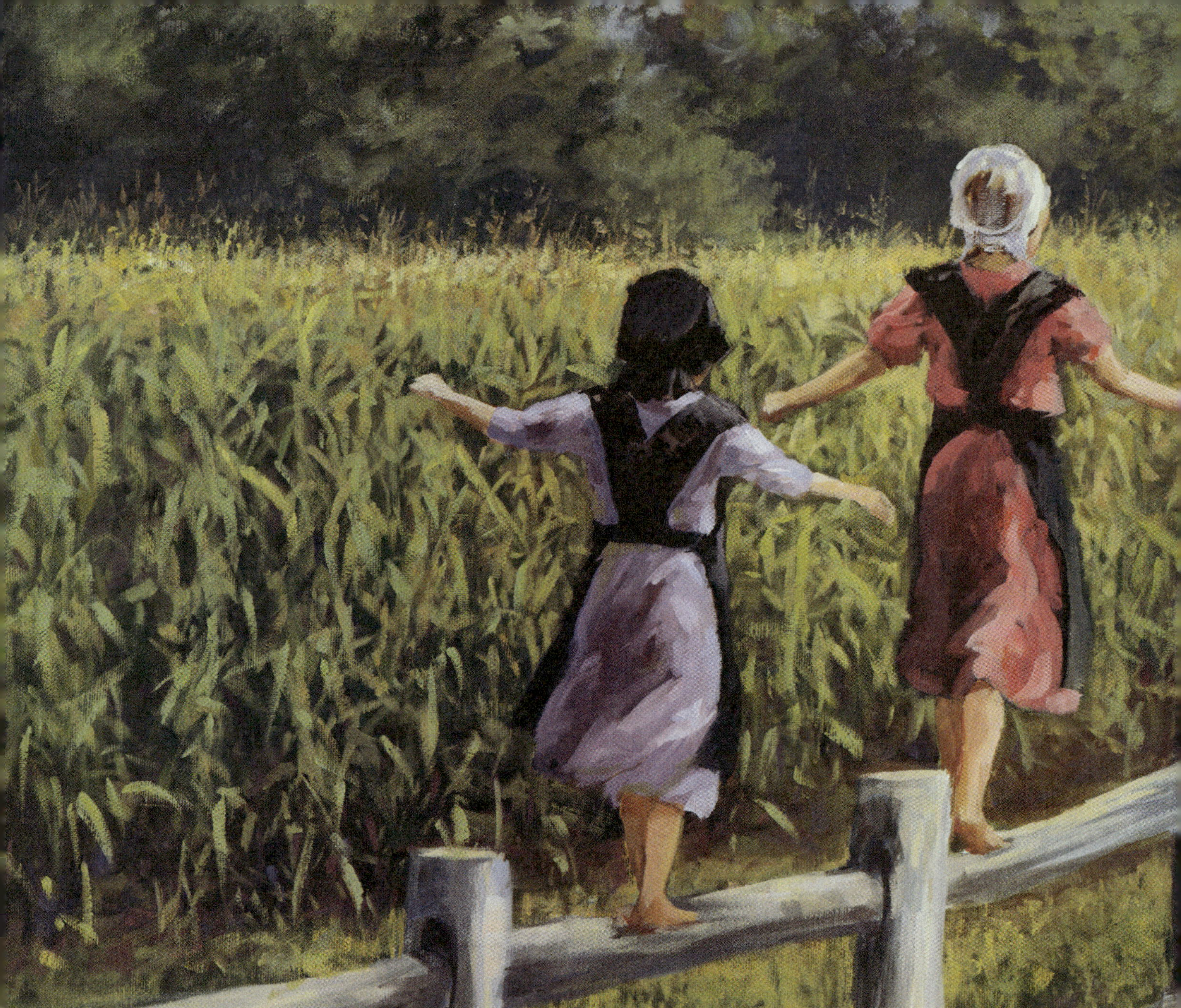

Sounds for a Child

Grace V. Watkins

O Lord of life, that every child
May have these memories: a field
Where he has heard a brook with slow,
Sweet-murmuring adagio,
In summer nights the largo sound
Of a little honeysuckle wind,

A mother's voice that sings a hymn
When vesper time is blue and dim,
A father's voice that reads the fair
Eternal Word and offers prayer,
A singing, shining certainty
Of faith more vast than any sea.

Children follow a fence into a summer day in GIRLS CAN TOO *by artist Laurie Snow Hein. Image copyright © Arts Uniq, Inc., Cookeville, Tennessee.*

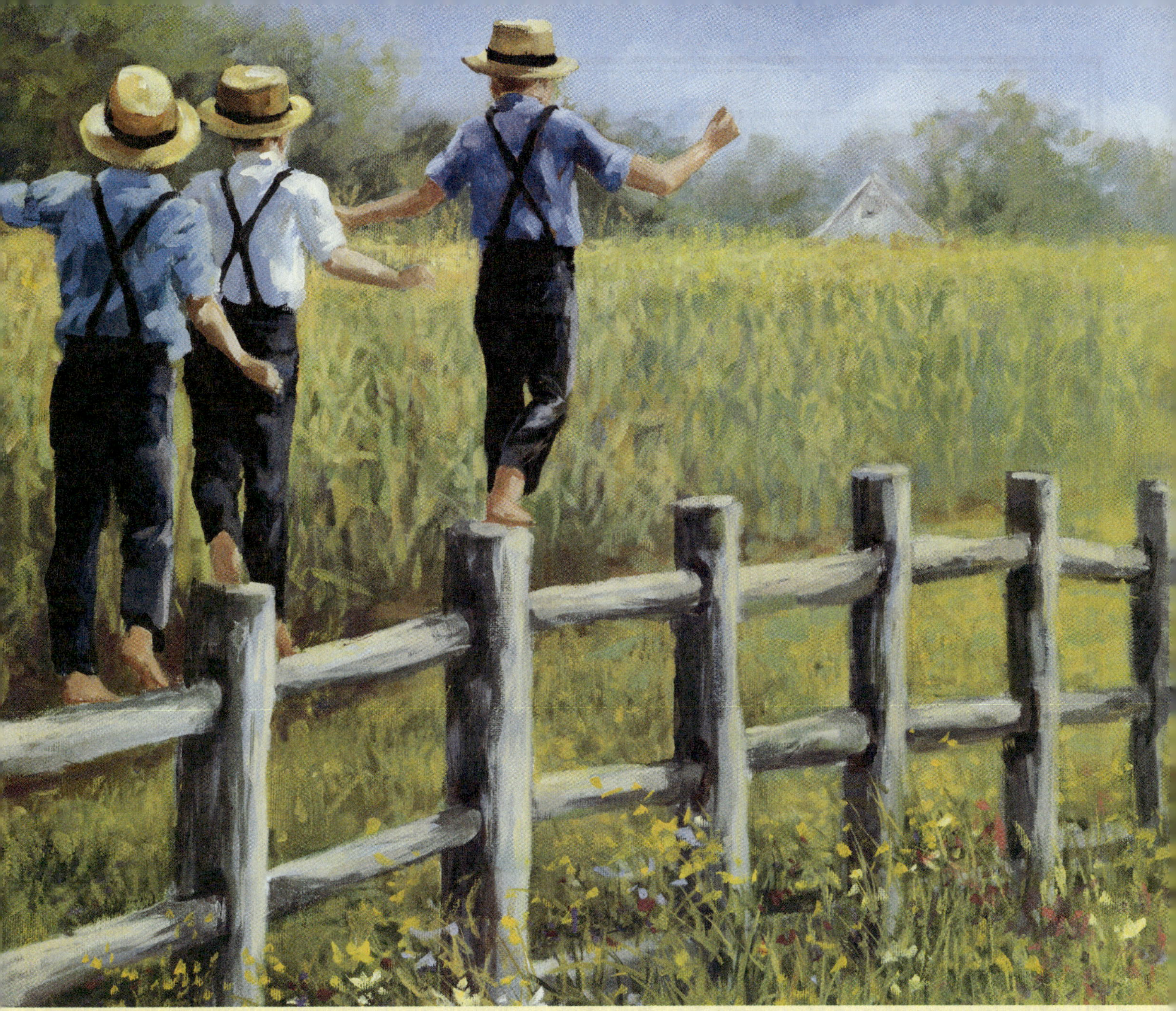

Legacy to a Son

Jessie Cannon Eldridge

I leave you a tangled field,
A gray-gnarled old elm tree,
A purple-misted far-off hill,
A river running free,
A weathered house with slanted roof,
Tall flowers set along
A winding walk,
Two apple trees,
The robins' welcome song,
The sparrows' nests built in the eaves,
Their morning twitterings,
A tall and fragrant lilac hedge,
Each new springtime that brings
Hope to a winter-laden heart,
Peace when the day is through.
The gatherings of a lifetime home
Are what I leave to you.

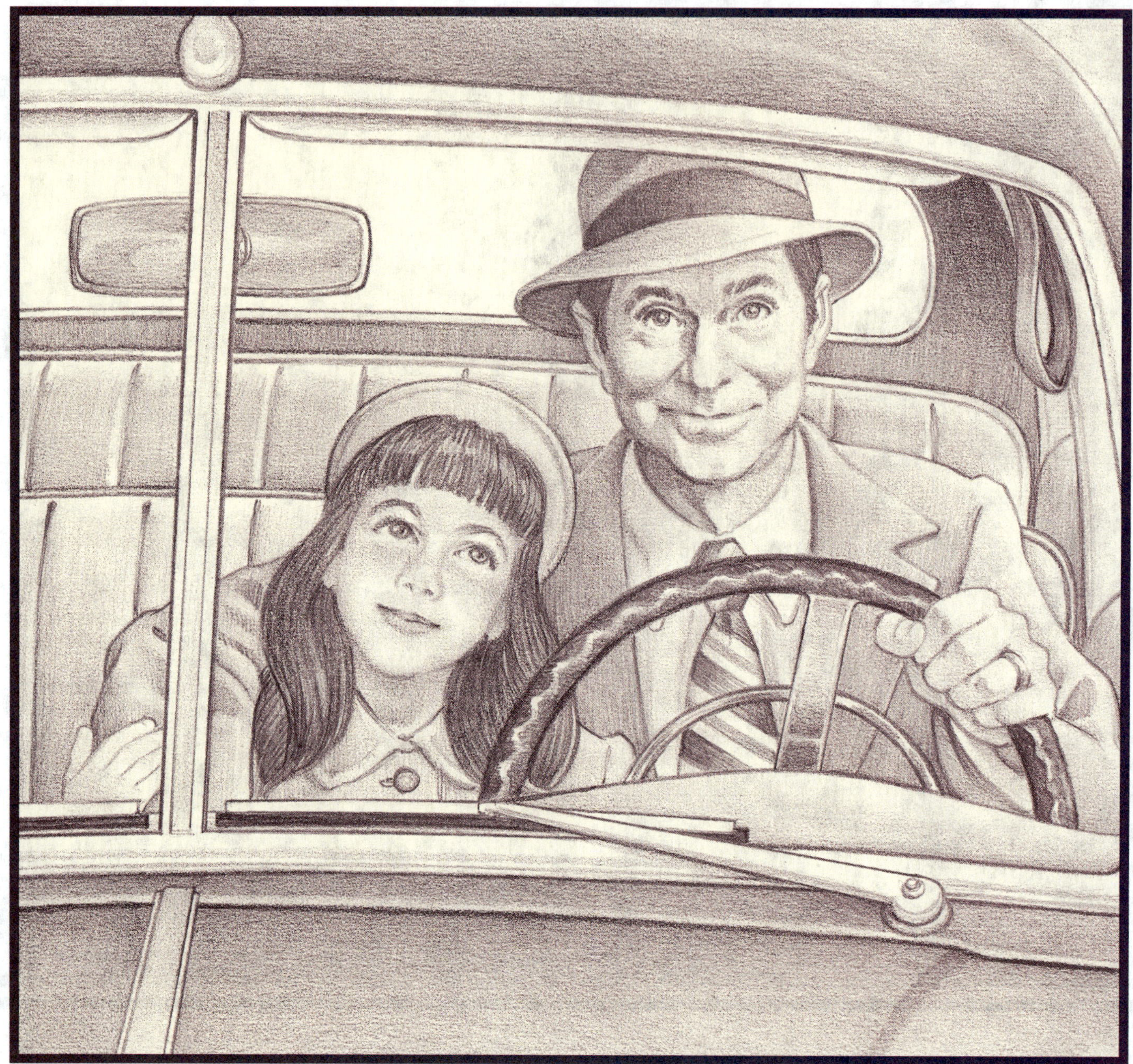

Fatherly Duties and Why I Love Them

Todd Wilson

It was one of those nights when I love being a dad. There I was, staring into the black night, blinded by the headlights of the oncoming traffic. I refused to blink, tightened my grip on the steering wheel, and resolved to get us through. The only noise I heard was the hypnotic sound of car tires on the pavement and an occasional grunt from my wife. We had traveled all day and now into the night. My wife sat slumped over in the seat next to mine fast asleep, which explains why she was grunting.

In the rearview mirror were the still figures of our children surrounded by the toys and books that we had brought along. Sam, the eldest, slept peacefully despite dried ketchup around his mouth and over his eyebrow. Ben, who has more energy in his little finger than I have in my whole body, was the last to succumb to the lull of the road. Kat, who hadn't stopped talking for the last ten hours, was now sucking hard on her thumb. Ike, the baby, was in his car seat sleeping.

I was tired and spent from a day of driving; yet in that moment of quiet exhaustion, a feeling of deep satisfaction grew within me. I was doing what dads were created to do. My family was sleeping, and I was protecting, guarding, and cherishing. They rested, and I worked. They slept unconcerned, and I wrestled over which exit to take. They rested because I was at the wheel. They trusted me and expected me to do my job.

Driving the family is my job, as it was my dad's before me. Not long ago I was the one who slept while he manned the wheel. The road noise was just as hypnotic then as it is now. On one occasion, I can remember a long day of driving to some place like North Carolina or Florida. We had consumed a couple hundred peanut butter and jelly sandwiches and had played every travel game conceived by man; and my dad had threatened to pull over at least every twenty or thirty miles. As the sun set, a stillness invaded the car until, one by one, my mom, siblings, and I fell asleep. Yet Dad drove on through the night.

I can remember more than once being awakened from sleep by some passing truck or pothole in the road. Through the dim light of traffic, I'd see the dark forms of my brothers, sister, and mom slumped in their seats. In the driver's seat, staring at black road, was my dad, quietly doing what we all expected him to do. I'd sit in the silence and watch my dad as a sailor might watch the captain at the helm during a storm. He never seemed to tire; yet looking back, I know he must have been exhausted. He never complained or asked my mother to relieve him of his post. After all, he was the dad.

I'd sit in the silence and watch my dad as a sailor might watch the captain at the helm during a storm.

The best part of those long nights was when we arrived at our destination. Dad stopped the car, turned off the engine, and then did what countless other dads have done down through the ages. He carried his children, one by one, to their beds. There were times when I had no idea how I arrived in bed; but on other occasions I pretended to be asleep and tried not to smile, just so Dad would carry me. I felt safe, protected, and cherished. I trusted him as my own children now trust me. I never dreamed that Dad might have liked it; but I bet he did, because I do.

On those late nights in the car, I sometimes imagine that I'm driving my squeaky Conestoga wagon up some treacherous mountain trail as my wife and young'uns sleep peacefully in the back, unaware of the possibility of grizzly attacks, rock slides, and missed exits. It's my job to keep them safe.

I am the protector. I am the shepherd of the little flock that God has entrusted to me. That's why I'm the first one out of the basement after a tornado warning has passed, and that's why I shovel the driveway when the wind howls its twenty-below-zero breath.

I will drive when others sleep. I will work while my family plays. I will stay alert when they are unaware. I will risk frostbite as they sit by the fire, and I will eat the heels while they eat the rest of the loaf. I will drive through the night as my wife and children sleep away the miles. I'll carry in the luggage and my children even if I see them trying hard not to smile. I won't give two hoots if they forget to thank me because I'm the dad; and I love doing it, especially for them.

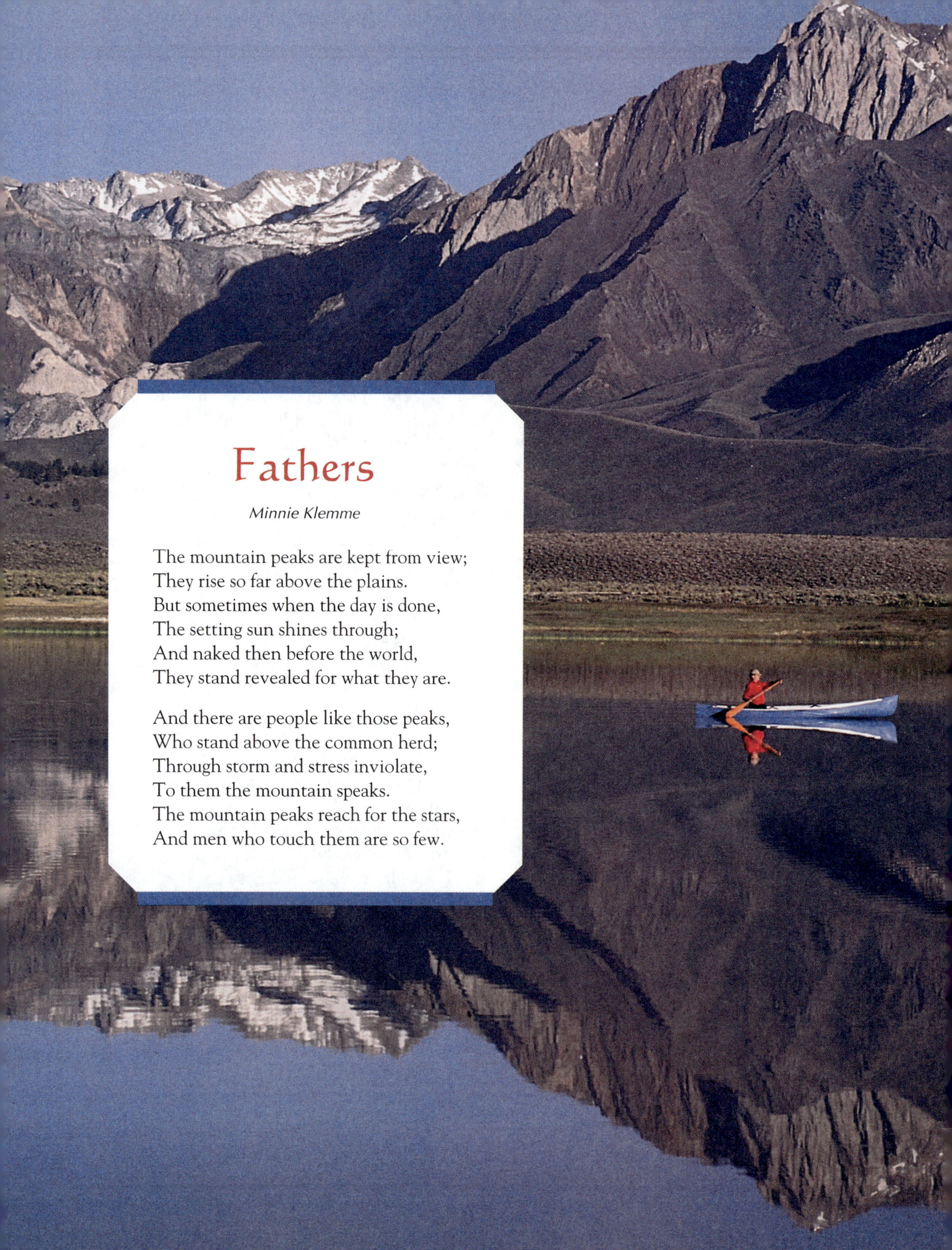

Fathers

Minnie Klemme

The mountain peaks are kept from view;
They rise so far above the plains.
But sometimes when the day is done,
The setting sun shines through;
And naked then before the world,
They stand revealed for what they are.

And there are people like those peaks,
Who stand above the common herd;
Through storm and stress inviolate,
To them the mountain speaks.
The mountain peaks reach for the stars,
And men who touch them are so few.

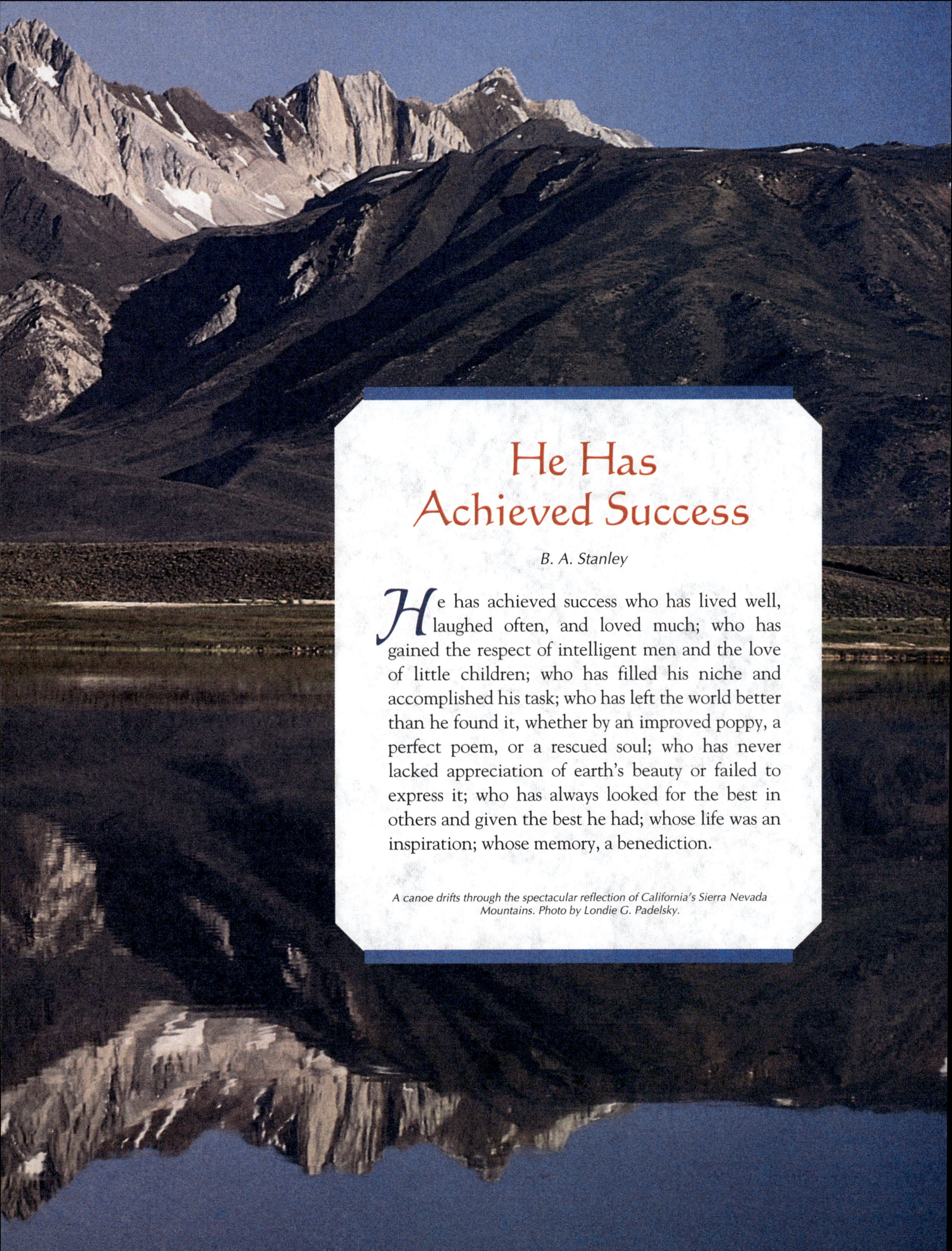

He Has Achieved Success

B. A. Stanley

He has achieved success who has lived well, laughed often, and loved much; who has gained the respect of intelligent men and the love of little children; who has filled his niche and accomplished his task; who has left the world better than he found it, whether by an improved poppy, a perfect poem, or a rescued soul; who has never lacked appreciation of earth's beauty or failed to express it; who has always looked for the best in others and given the best he had; whose life was an inspiration; whose memory, a benediction.

A canoe drifts through the spectacular reflection of California's Sierra Nevada Mountains. Photo by Londie G. Padelsky.

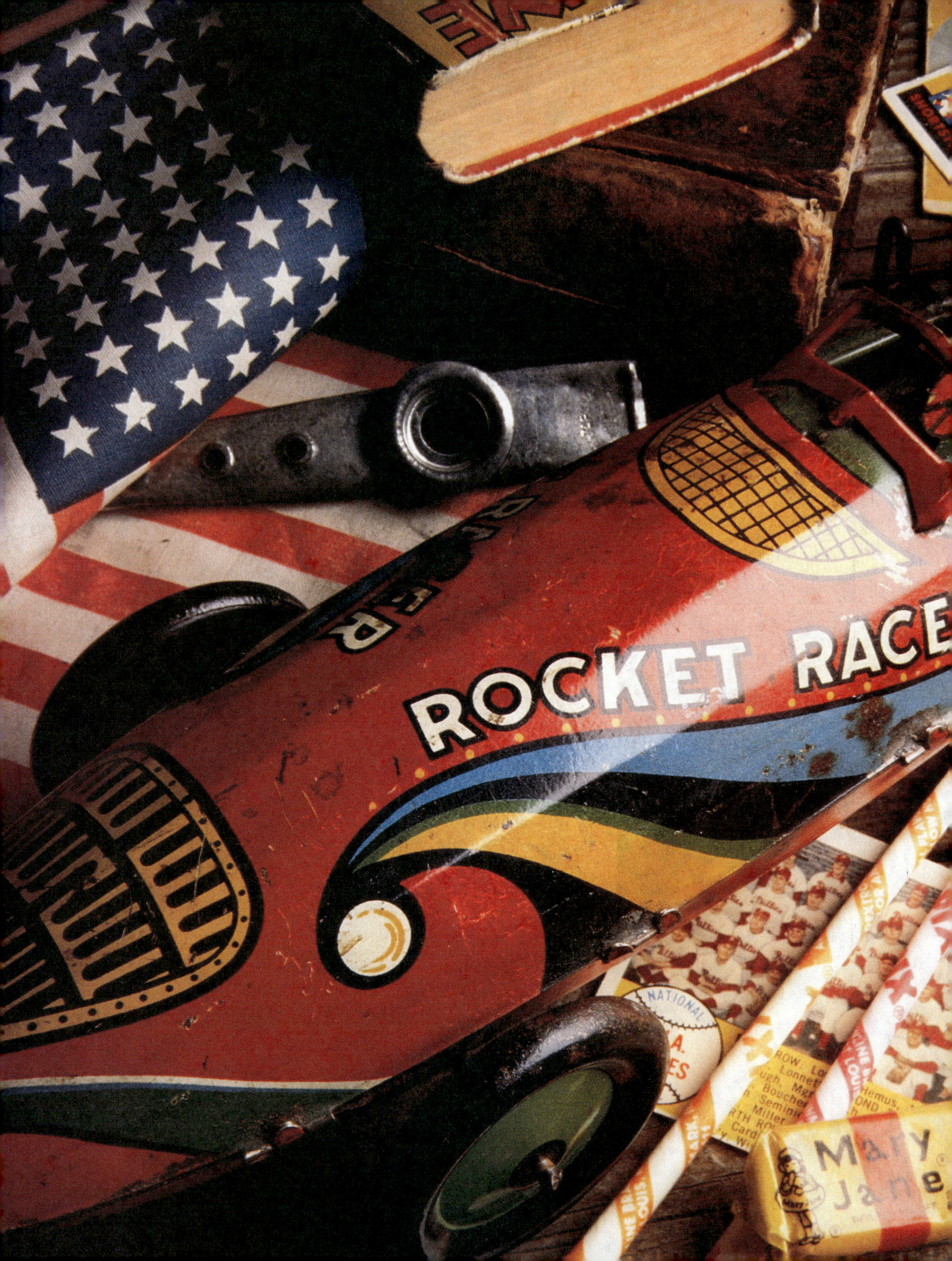
ROCKET RACE
Mary Jane

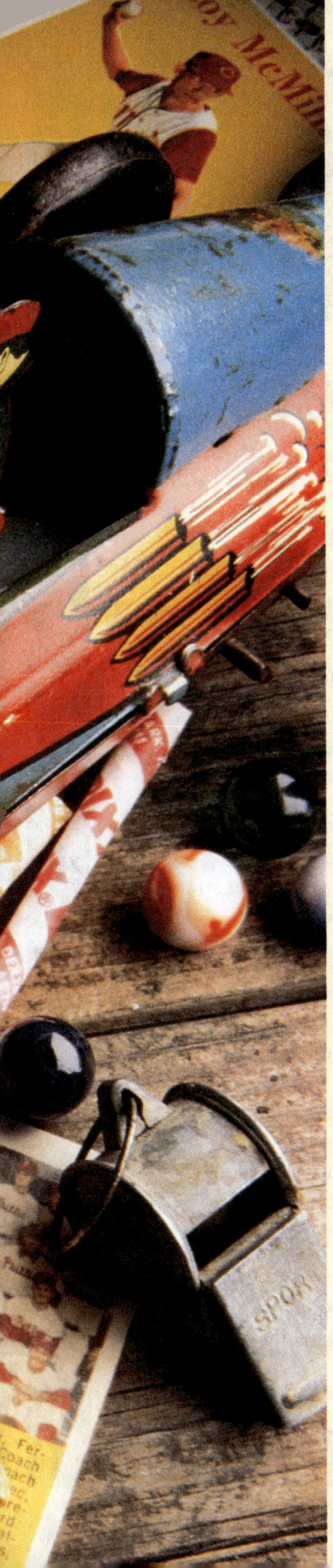

To My Little Boy

Author Unknown

How often as I watch you at your play
I wish that, through the years, you might remain
A boy, as now upon a summer's day,
Changeless and glad and unaware of pain.
Your laughter falls with sadness in my heart.
It is so young, so sure, so unafraid;
You have not heard there is a time to part
Or that the road leads down into the shade.

Would I might keep from you what all must learn—
The doubt, the fever, battles lost and wild.
Would I might build a world that does not turn
To dust beneath the footsteps of a child!
Darling, that this can never be I know,
Yet it is out of earth that flowers grow.

What Are Little Boys Made Of?

Mary Richstone

Snips and snails and puppy dog tails?
Certainly not! These miniature males
Are made of wonder and stubborn pride
And chuckles and good clean dirt from outside.
They are made of sweetness that's nine-tenths guile
And mischief redeemed by an angelic smile.
They are made of curiosity and devotion,
But mostly they're made of perpetual motion.

A tabletop brims with a young boy's treasures. Photo by Gerg Strelecki/International Stock.

The Field

Glenn Ward Dresbach

I stand again in the field
Where first my father broke
The prairie sod, and the sweating team
Passed with the creak of yoke
And straining tug, and steam
Arose from the furrows that rolled,
Tough and straight and black,
under the morning's gold.

Many times he has said
He remembers, each spring that comes,
The wildflowers and the steady roll
Of the prairie chicken drums
Upon each sunny knoll,
And how the tall grass sighed
As it fell beneath share
and his relentless stride.

Sometimes I wish I had known
The field when it was wild
And beautiful, but remembered then,
Although my father smiled
When he told of it again,
He had lost a treasured thing—
Something he wished to keep,
and kept remembering.

A Simple Man

Helen Turnbull Phelps

My dad—
A simple man is he,
Who tills the fertile soil,
With only faith to guarantee
The fruitlings of his toil.

He views with pride the tender shoots
From seeds which he has sown,
And smells the spicy summer tang
Of clover hay, new-mown.

Both flood and drought he takes in stride
As setbacks, nothing more,
And somewhere finds that inner strength
To start his planting o'er.

He sees the radiant streaks of dawn
Break o'er his greening fields
And, undismayed, looks forward to
Abundant harvest yields.

And though he toils from dawn to dusk,
It seems a worthwhile task.
He claims a partnership with God—
What more could mortal ask?

He wouldn't trade his kind of work
For any else on earth,
'Cause farmers have that in-born faith
That's pre-ordained at birth.

A stream meanders through a barnyard in Calumet County, Wisconsin. Photo by Darryl R. Beers.

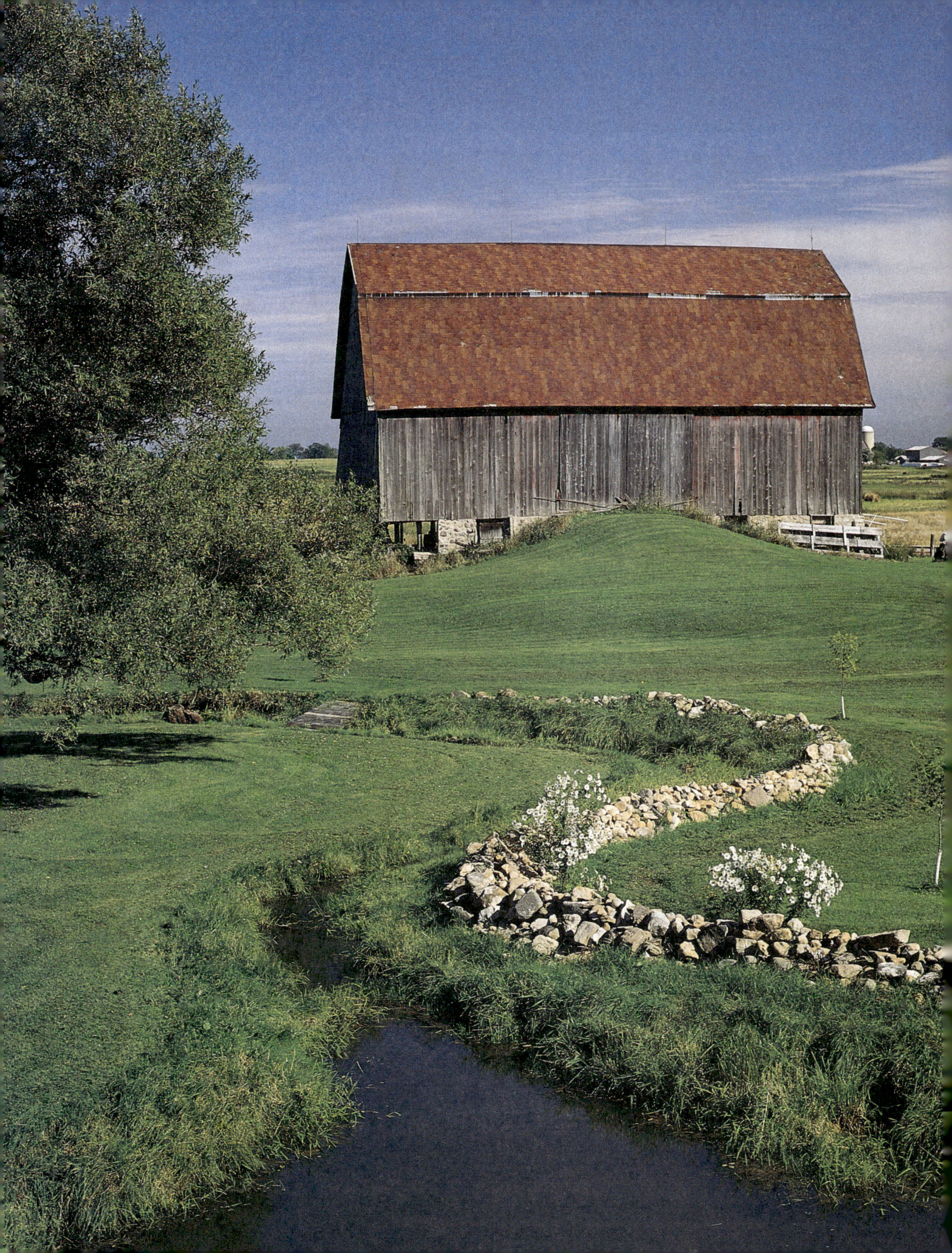

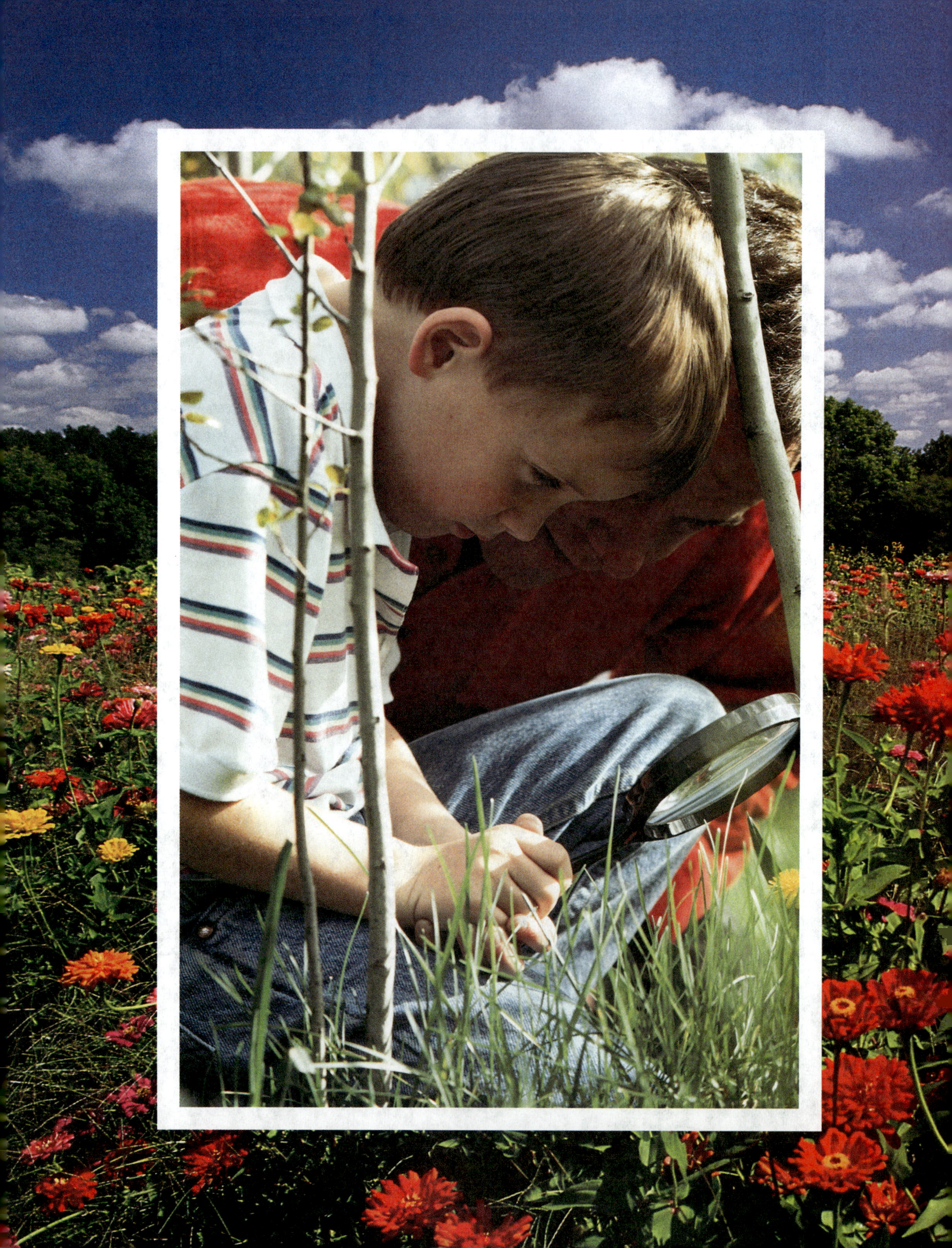

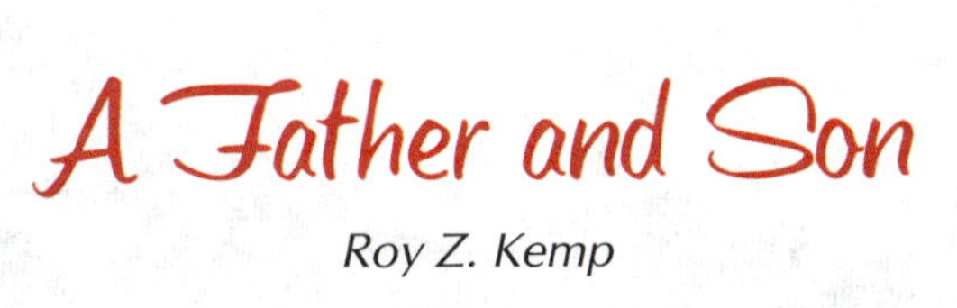

A Father and Son

Roy Z. Kemp

He towered over me when I was small
Like some great giant: rugged, high, and tall,
Obscuring from me half the skies
Because of his great body, arms, and thighs.

I did not mind; I loved this big, tall man
In all the loving ways a small child can.
And when he swung me up high into space
And pressed me close, and when his beaming face

Was brought close to my own, it was delight;
It was rapture made of joy and fright.
The ground seemed far away, close were the skies,
And heaven's glory shone within his eyes.

Then I grew up and he seemed to grow down,
For I became the tallest man in town.
I still look up to him from high above,
And still the eyes of both of us show love.

Inset: A father shares his son's small discoveries. Photo by Superstock.
Border: A field of zinnias glows in the summer sun. Photo by Gay Bumgarner.

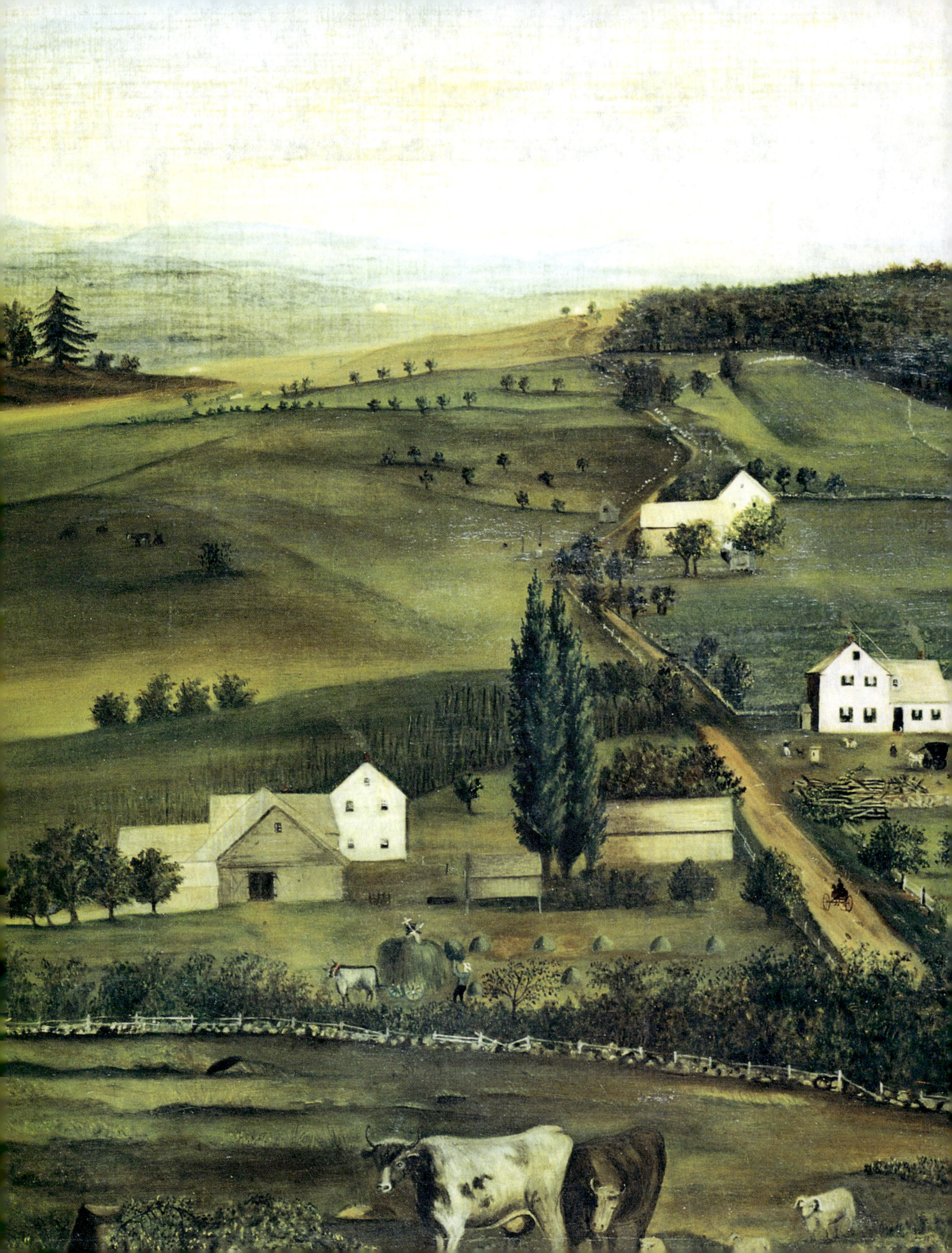

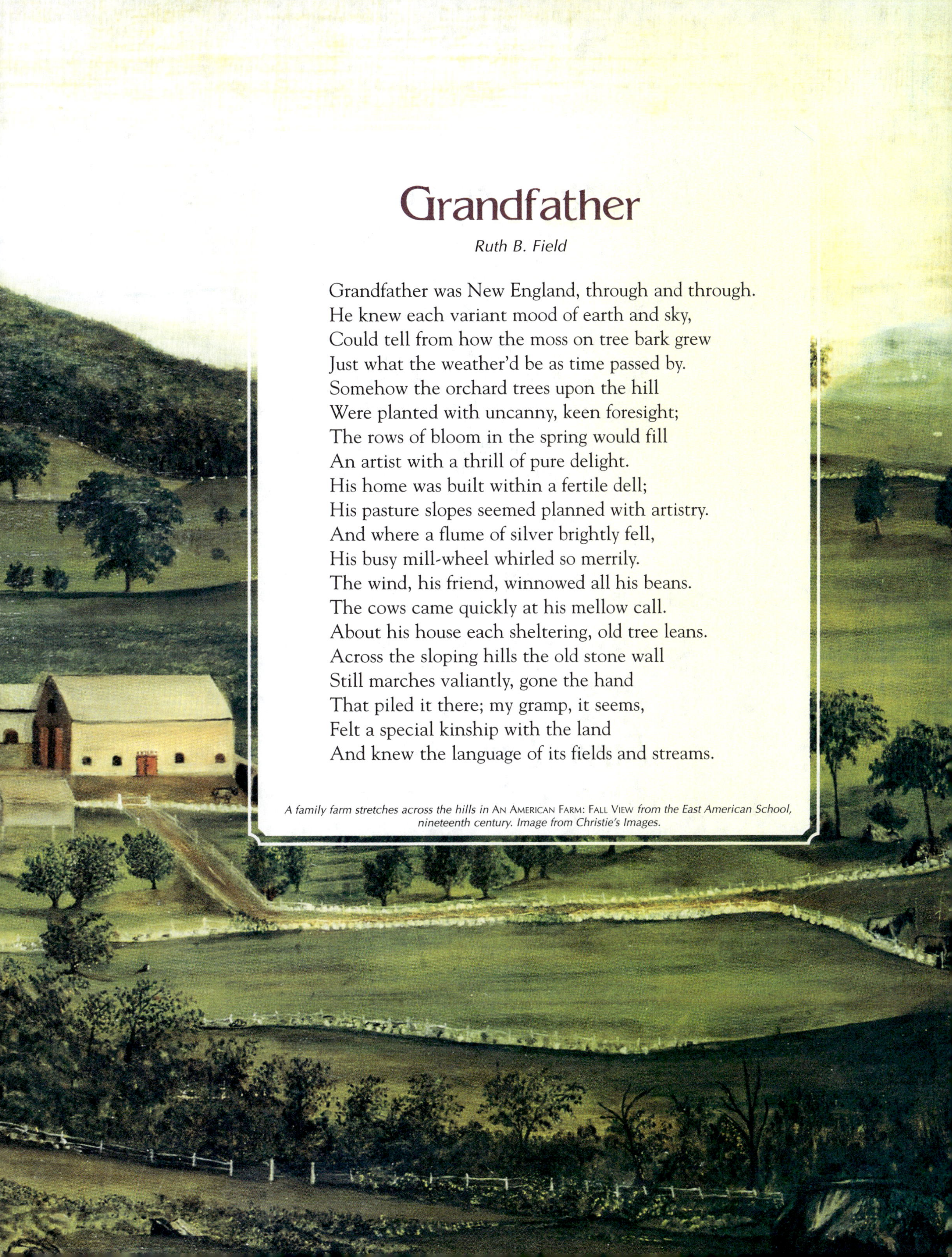

Grandfather

Ruth B. Field

Grandfather was New England, through and through.
He knew each variant mood of earth and sky,
Could tell from how the moss on tree bark grew
Just what the weather'd be as time passed by.
Somehow the orchard trees upon the hill
Were planted with uncanny, keen foresight;
The rows of bloom in the spring would fill
An artist with a thrill of pure delight.
His home was built within a fertile dell;
His pasture slopes seemed planned with artistry.
And where a flume of silver brightly fell,
His busy mill-wheel whirled so merrily.
The wind, his friend, winnowed all his beans.
The cows came quickly at his mellow call.
About his house each sheltering, old tree leans.
Across the sloping hills the old stone wall
Still marches valiantly, gone the hand
That piled it there; my gramp, it seems,
Felt a special kinship with the land
And knew the language of its fields and streams.

A family farm stretches across the hills in AN AMERICAN FARM: FALL VIEW *from the East American School, nineteenth century. Image from Christie's Images.*

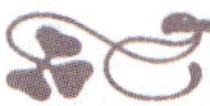
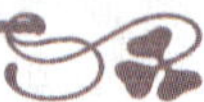

Small Boy on a Horse

Harry Elmore Hurd

The work of day is done
Beneath the whirling sun.

The final load of hay
Fills the upper bay.

The horses clatter free
From the whippletree.

This is the hour of joy
For the farmer boy

Who, climbing from the rack,
Mounts the nigh-horse's back.

The team-horse, glad to follow,
Follows to the hollow;

The thirsty horses drink
At the clear brook's brink.

The crystal water flows
Around each sloshing nose.

The horses drink their fill
Then gallop up the hill—

Through the great barn door.
The boy slides to the floor

With a shout of glee
And strips each harness free,

Pegs them on the wall,
Then spanks each horse to stall.

Who knows a greater joy
Than this farmer boy?

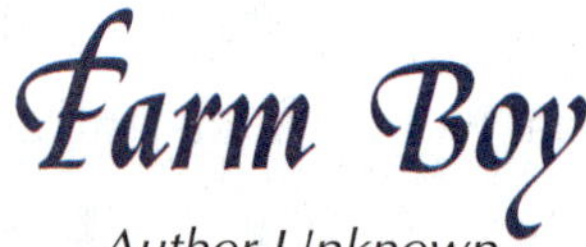

Farm Boy

Author Unknown

He walks the fields light shod, carefree,
His frame bespeaking energy.
His mind is stayed on black, rich sod,
Attuned to nature, things of God.
His treasures lie in wholesome breeze,
In azure skies and spreading trees;
His heart lifts up as birds on wing,
And all creation crowns him king.

Two young friends share the meadow in Kathryn Andrews Fincher's HOWDY PARTNER. *Image copyright © Arts Uniq, Inc., Cookeville, Tennessee.*

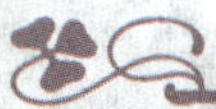
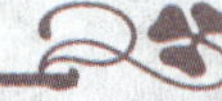

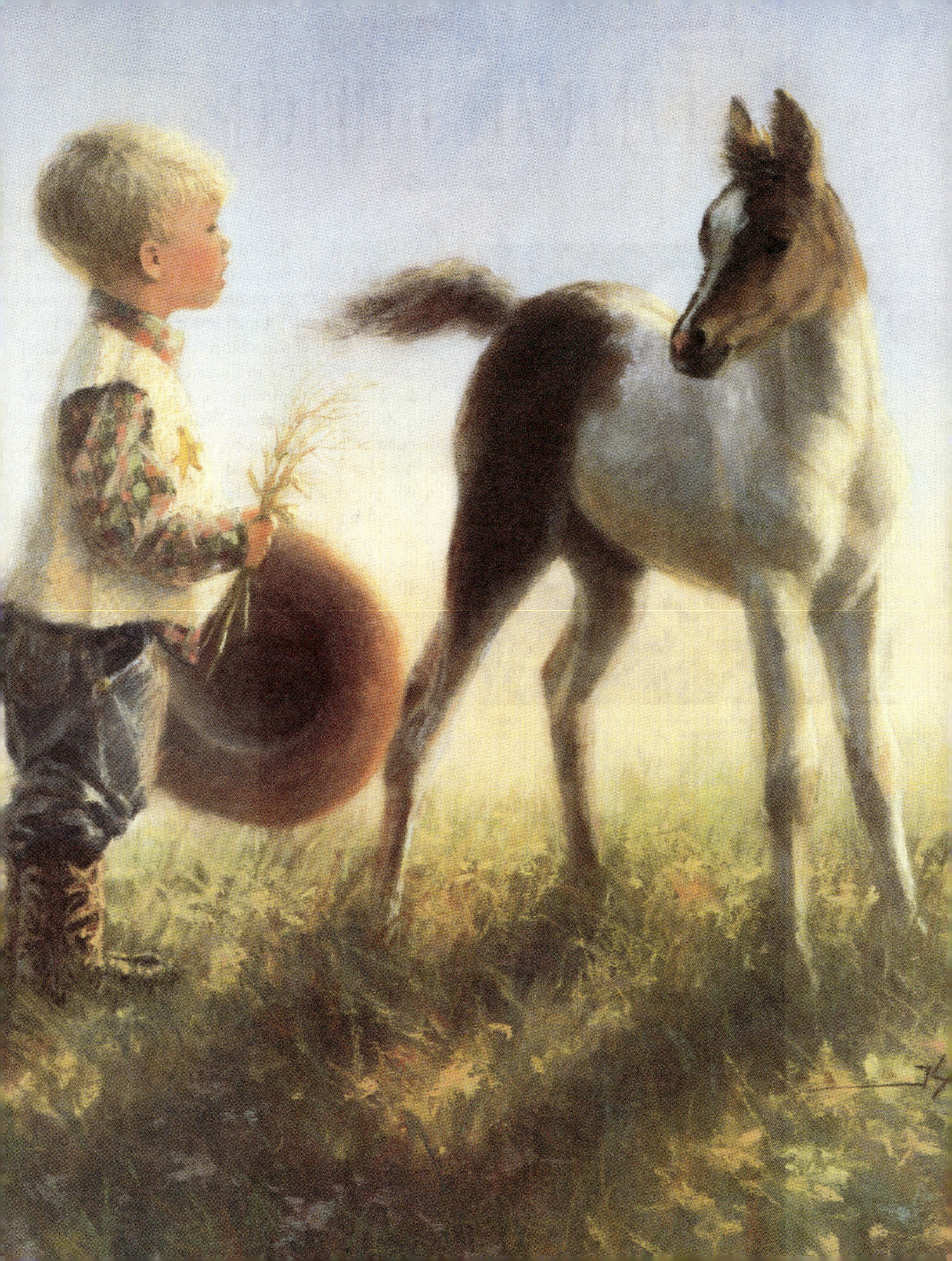

Handmade Heirloom

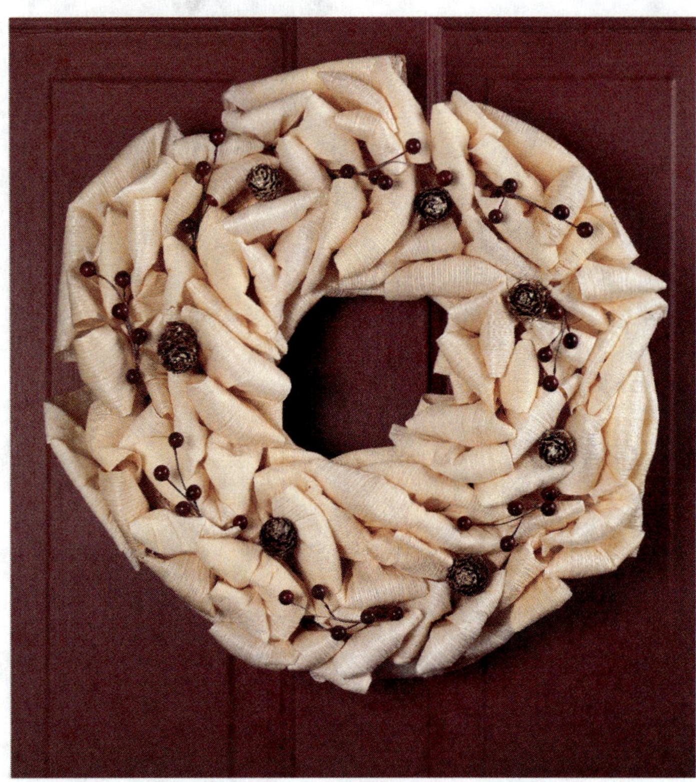

Above and opposite: Handmade cornhusk wreaths add a touch of the country to an urban home. Wreaths crafted by Lisa Ragan. Photo by Jerry Koser.

Cornhusk Wreath

Lisa Ragan

Corn has been a part of my life as long as I can remember. As a native of Indiana, I grew up in the Corn Belt, which meant I learned some important facts of life at an early age. For example, I learned that "knee high by the fourth of July" referred to the height of those waving fields of green corn past which I rode my bike on lazy summer afternoons. Most importantly, however, I knew Indiana sweet corn was the best-tasting corn in the world. At least so it seemed to me at age ten, barefoot and ponytailed, sitting at the picnic table in my backyard.

Teenagers in my hometown often worked summers picking corn, husking corn, and cleaning corn; it was hot, dirty work for little pay. Forever with my nose in a book, I dreamed of going to the old-fashioned husking bees that I had read about so I could do-si-do to the fiddle music after all the corn had been husked. But alas, no one organized husking bees once the farm machinery and teenagers took over. Another thing I read about those husking bees, however, was that the women often kept the shucked cornhusks to use later in a variety of ways. They made brooms, doormats, woven chair seats, mattress stuffing, dolls, and wreaths. Cornhusk brooms were so popular, in fact, that a particular variety of corn, aptly named broom corn, could be grown specifically for making brooms from the husks.

Crafting wonderful creations from cornhusks began years ago with Native Americans. The indigenous peoples of America had known the remarkable qualities of maize, the corn plant, long before they presented gifts of corn to the European settlers. Native Americans not only valued the corn itself but also crafted the husks into moccasins, baskets, thatched roofs, masks, and dolls. After harvest celebrations, Iroquois women in particular often made cornhusk dolls for their children. Just as they taught European settlers and others how to grow and harvest corn, Native Americans also shared their creativity in using the spent husks. Today, Native Americans all across America, as well as artisans in the Appalachian Mountains, continue to fashion cornhusks into dolls, wreaths, and other objects now treasured as American folk art.

As for me, I recently crafted a few cornhusk wreaths to celebrate my own Corn Belt roots and my growing-up years in Indiana. Since I no longer reside near those waving fields of corn and there's nary a husking bee to be found, obtaining husks proved to be a challenge. First I began saving husks from the sweet corn I bought at the farmer's market, but I soon realized that this method would take too long. So I asked all of my friends to save their husks for me too. In the meantime I considered purchasing husks at the crafts store or in the Mexican-foods section of the grocery store (cornhusks are used to wrap tamales). I even contemplated driving out into the countryside to find a generous farmer who would provide me with husks, but I need not have worried. By the time I gathered all the husks that my friends had been saving for me, I had enough for many a wreath.

For my wreath, I chose sweet-corn husks, which tend to be whiter and more delicate, although field-corn husks can be used too. Some crafters consider the husks from sweet corn too small and fragile, whereas the tougher field-corn husks do work better for making sturdy baskets, mats, and the like. Field-corn husks can be bleached to whiten them, a process which also softens them. Some crafters prefer to use the husks from Indian corn, which often yields husks in subtle colors of brown, red, maroon, or pink.

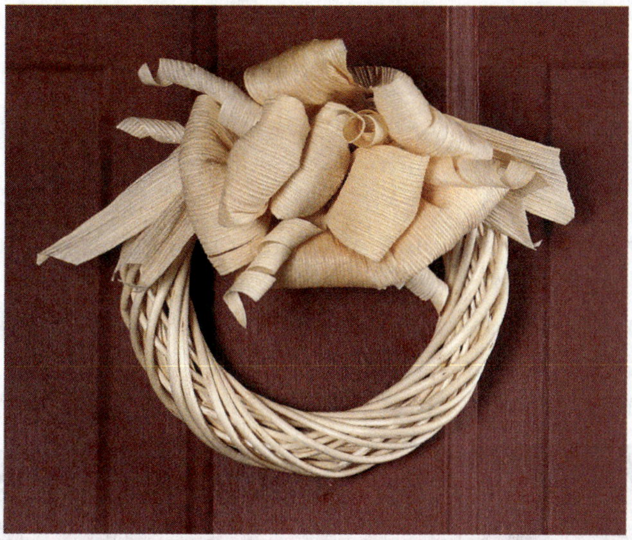

Because my husks were still green, I spread them out on newspapers for a few days to dry to a creamy white. Husks can also be dried by hanging them in the sun or in a mesh bag. Once dried, they can be bleached, softened, or dyed. To bleach cornhusks, add one-fourth cup liquid bleach to a half gallon of water and soak the husks for about a half hour; then rinse well. To soften unbleached cornhusks, either soak them in plain water or in a glycerin solution (add two or three teaspoons of glycerin to two quarts water). The glycerin solution increases the pliability of the husks, making them easier to fold and braid.

Dried cornhusks make stunning wreaths in their natural, creamy white hue but can also be dyed a variety of colors for unlimited design possibilities. Native American artisans tinted husks in subtle, earth tones by soaking them in solutions of beet juice, blueberries, grapes, marigolds, onion skins, turmeric, and even black walnut hulls. To use these natural dyes, crush the substance and soak it overnight before bringing it to a boil. Add a drop of dish detergent (to increase uniformity of color absorption) and soak the husks until they achieve the desired color. Husks can also be dyed with commercial fabric dye or food coloring. Prepare fabric dye according to manufacturer's instructions. Soak the husks until they appear a shade darker than desired. Rinse off the excess dye and scatter the husks on newspapers to dry. For one of my wreaths, I painted the husks with patriotic-colored fabric paint, which I brushed on slightly damp husks. I let the husks dry overnight to seal the color and then re-wet them to work into the wreath.

The husks must be kept damp while working them into the wreath. For my natural, cream-colored wreaths, I folded each damp husk in half and then secured the ends with florist's wire. I placed the fold on a straw wreath form and pinned it in place with a florist's pin. I continued adding folds until the wreath form was completely covered, and then I accented the wreath with a few gilded pinecones and artificial berries. I used similar folds for the bow on a small bent willow wreath. For the curlicues in the bow, I wrapped small strands of damp husk around a pencil and secured the ends with clothespins. When the husks were dry, I added the curlicues to the bow with a hot glue gun. For the patriotic wreath, I layered folds of damp husks (which I had already colored with fabric paint) around a straw wreath form and secured with florist's pins.

Cornhusk wreaths make ideal outdoor decorations since the husks naturally resist rain and snow and can be rinsed off as needed to clean. When damp, the husks are surprisingly hardy and can be braided, woven, curled, knotted, twisted, or wrapped. If the dried result is not quite right, the husks can be simply re-wet and reshaped. Although cornhusks can be worked into a variety of crafts, they are not suitable for lampshades or candleholders because the husks do burn easily.

My wreaths now decorate the front of my little urban bungalow and remind me of carefree summer days growing up in Indiana. I can close my eyes and picture the fields of corn stretching for miles over the flat terrain. I think about my European and Native American ancestors and the important role corn played in their lives. To me, my wreaths represent a deep patriotic spirit, an American heirloom born from the very heart of our country.

TRAVELER'S *Diary*

Corn Palace
Mitchell, South Dakota

Christine Landry

While making corn soup recently, I was reminded of a cross-country trip I once took that included a stop at Mitchell, South Dakota, the home of the world's only Corn Palace. As someone who enjoys cooking, I normally view corn as nutritious and appetizing and often use it in casseroles, chowders, and muffins. And I have fond childhood memories of Thanksgiving plays where I dressed up as a small pilgrim and received a gift of corn from another young actor. When I visited Mitchell, however, I realized that my view of corn was quite limited; for there corn takes center stage on a palace whose exterior is adorned with fantastic designs and murals, all created from grass, grain, and corn.

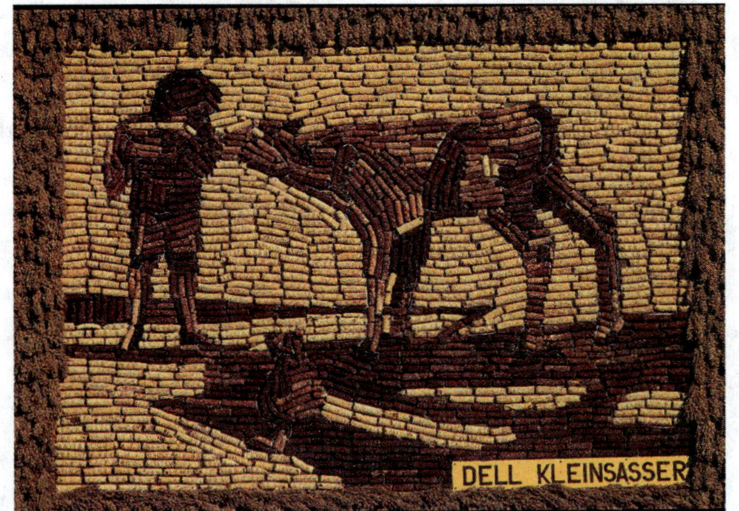

A detail of one of the mosaics reveals the number of ears of corn used to create it. Photo by Jessie Walker.

When planning my cross-country journey, I decided that I would stop along the way not only to visit world-famous sites like the Grand Canyon, but also to visit small towns with places of interest that would add some local color to my trip. One of these stops included the Corn Palace, a place I was impressed to discover entertains more than 400,000 visitors every year.

The Corn Palace was originally built in 1892 in Mitchell, a city that then only consisted of three thousand people. The building was established to hold the Corn Belt Exposition (later renamed the Corn Palace Festival) for local residents. The landmark was also intended to display the bounty of the local soil. The celebration has become a tradition that has only been canceled by extenuating circumstances, such as extreme drought or economic depression. In 1905 the original building was replaced, and in 1921 a new, larger building was built on Fifth and Main and the second building was torn down. This is the site of today's Corn Palace.

The base of the 125-by-145-foot structure is a long rectangular shape, and visitors initially complained that it lacked the majestic grandeur of the previous building. For this reason, minarets, turrets, and kiosks were added to the building to give it more of a castle-like appearance. I could still see the brick foundation of the building, but I was amazed to see that the majority of the structure was covered in corn.

Each September, the palace is redecorated, with the previous year's corn replaced and new designs displayed from the most recent crop. These decorations are always all natural and consist of nine different colors of corn, such as red, purple, yellow, white, and calico, which depict a chosen theme for that

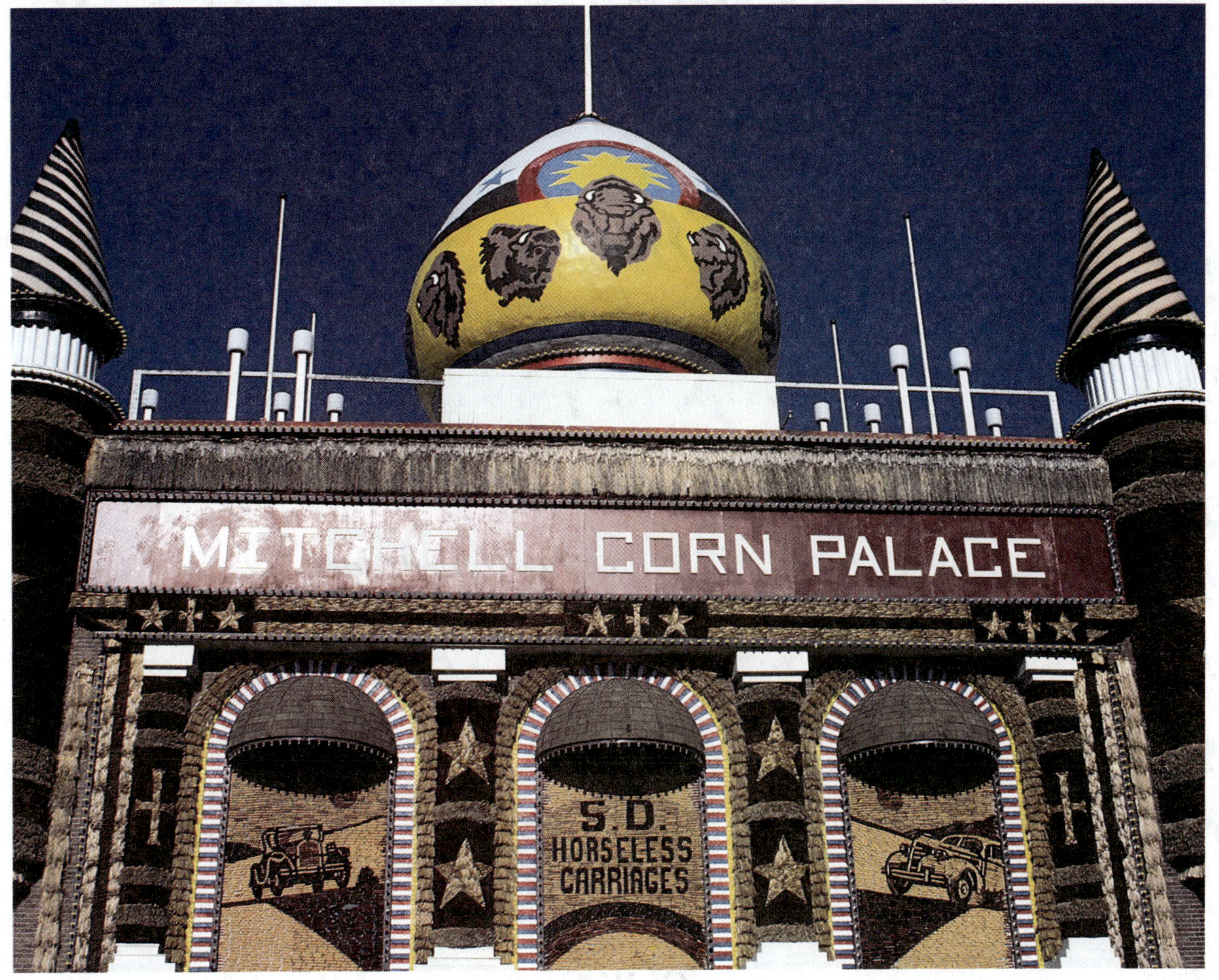

Paintings and mosaics by local artists cover almost all of the Corn Palace's ornate exterior. Photo by Gay Bumgarner.

year. The process typically requires thousands of bushels of corn, grain, and grass and costs over $100,000. This is all part of a long-standing Mitchell tradition that has evolved over the years into a huge celebration of South Dakota's land and heritage.

When I viewed the Corn Palace, the murals featured Native Americans looking across the plains, wolves framed by moonlight, wagons traveling across vast yellow landscapes, and tepees huddled together. Other themes have included "Salute to Agriculture," "Nights and Fables," and "South Dakota Fauna." During World War II, the Corn Palace displayed oil paintings of war scenes rather than create them out of corn, since corn was a much-needed food supply. South Dakotan artists are usually selected to design the images which will appear on the outside of the building. The artists create miniature drawings that are then duplicated on the walls of the building with corn.

Walking through the streets of Mitchell during the festival, I was able to enjoy rides and agricultural displays. I also snacked on some popcorn and attended a concert inside the Corn Palace, which serves as an auditorium as well as a basketball court for the local high school. Upon leaving Mitchell, I was inspired by the vibrancy of this small town and the pride the residents have in their state's history. No longer will I view corn as just simple nourishment, but as a reminder of our country's rich heritage and bountiful blessings.

Ideals'

Family Recipes

The next time your neighbors share an overflowing basket of corn from their latest crop, try one of these favorite dishes. Just be sure to set aside enough ears for some buttered corn on the cob too; what would summer be without it? We would love to try your favorite family recipe. Send a typed copy to Ideals Publications, 535 Metroplex Drive, Suite 250, Nashville, TN 37211. *We pay $10 for each recipe published.*

Deluxe Scalloped Corn

Trenette Hite of Fargo, North Dakota

- *1 8½-ounce box corn muffin mix*
- *½ cup butter, melted*
- *1 egg, beaten*
- *1 cup sour cream*
- *1 14¾-ounce can cream-style corn*
- *1 15¼-ounce can whole kernel corn with liquid*

Preheat oven to 350° F. In a large mixing bowl, combine all ingredients; mix well. Pour mixture into an 11-by-7-inch greased baking pan. Bake 45 minutes. Makes 8 servings.

Chili Corn Casserole

Hannah G. Kellerby of Cody, Wyoming

- *1 14¾-ounce can cream-style corn*
- *¼ cup vegetable oil*
- *¼ cup cornmeal*
- *1 egg, beaten*
- *¼ teaspoon garlic salt*
- *¼ teaspoon salt*
- *1 4-ounce can green chili peppers, diced and drained*
- *½ cup shredded Cheddar cheese*

Preheat oven to 350° F. In a large mixing bowl, combine corn and oil. Add cornmeal, egg, garlic salt, and salt and mix well. Stir in chili peppers and half of cheese. Spoon batter into a lightly greased, glass, 1-quart baking dish and sprinkle with remaining cheese. Bake 1 hour or until browned. Makes 6 servings.

Corn Pudding

Joyce Elaine Boring of Schwenksville, Pennsylvania

- *3 eggs*
- *1 tablespoon granulated sugar*
- *1 tablespoon all-purpose flour*
- *3 tablespoons butter, melted*
- *1½ teaspoons salt*
- *1⅓ cups warmed milk*
- *¼ cup diced onion*
- *1½ cups whole kernel corn*

Preheat oven to 350° F. Place eggs in a blender and process until beaten. Add remaining ingredients, processing until corn is thoroughly mixed into batter. Pour batter into a greased 1½-quart baking dish. Bake 1 hour and 10 minutes or until firm. Makes 6 servings.

Corn Chowder

Barb Marshall of Pickerington, Ohio

- *2 cups peeled, cubed potatoes*
- *½ cup cooked bacon, crumbled*
- *1 medium onion, diced*
- *1 tablespoon butter*
- *2 cups cream-style corn*
- *1 12-ounce can evaporated milk*
- *Salt and pepper to taste*

In a large saucepan, cover potatoes with water and bring to a boil. Cook potatoes 25 to 30 minutes or until tender; do not drain. Set aside. In a medium skillet, sauté onion in butter until golden. Add onion, bacon, corn, milk, and salt and pepper to potatoes. Mix well. Heat through; serve immediately. Makes 6 to 8 servings.

Corn Salad

Emma Brown of Nashville, Tennessee

- *1 11-ounce can shoepeg corn, drained*
- *¼ cup diced onion*
- *½ red pepper, diced*
- *½ green pepper, diced*
- *1 stalk celery, diced*
- *2 tablespoons mayonnaise*
- *Salt and pepper to taste*

In a large bowl, combine all ingredients. Chill overnight. Makes 4 servings.

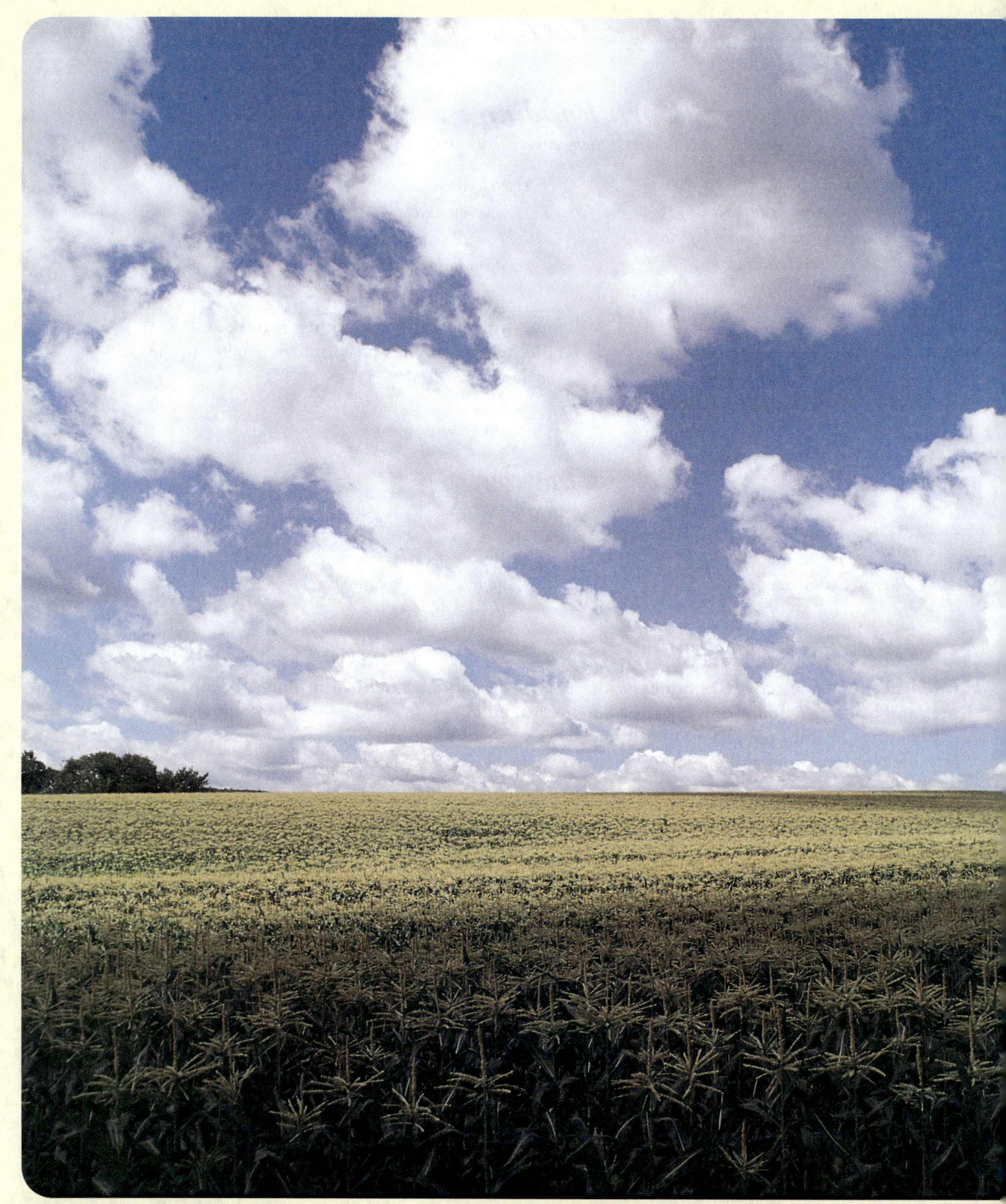

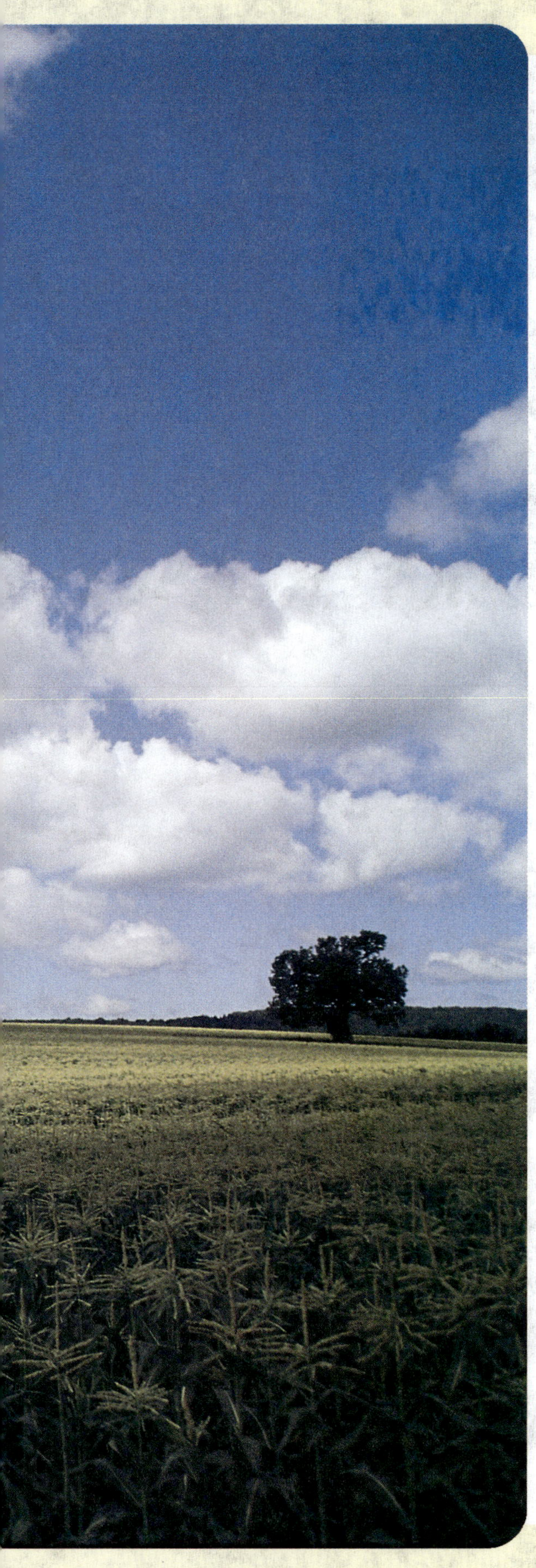

Corn

Sylvia Trent Auxier

Across the road there stands my field of corn
In ordered rows—from east to west they run.
Its green and lusty stalks are newly born
To earth and sky. They woo the brazen sun
By tossing playful tassels in the air
And reaching arms to catch her every beam.
By day her passionate embrace they share;
At night, in her remembered warmth, they dream.

The jealous clouds parade before the sun;
They bow and pose and often change their coat
From white to gray. No favors having won,
Against my field their shadow columns float.
Like hungry vultures, ponderous and slow,
They move, advance, maneuver, and retreat;
Blot out the corn, engulf it row by row—
Then move away in lowering defeat.

In ordered rows still stands my field of corn,
And in the shadowed soul new hope is born.

The full ripe corn is bending
In waves of golden light.
—Thomas J. Ouseley

A gold-topped field of corn meets the sky in America's heartland. Photo by Superstock.

Farmers' Market

Mary Louise Cheatham

Shoppers study and compare,
Buying foods in open air.
Apples, grapes, and rosy peaches,
Each fruit beckons and beseeches.

Beans, tomatoes, corn for roasting,
Box and basket, tempting, boasting.
Every purchase is a winner—
Food and beauty too for dinner!

I have often thought that if heaven had given me choice of my position and calling, it should have been on a rich spot of earth, well watered, and near a good market for the productions of the garden.

—Thomas Jefferson

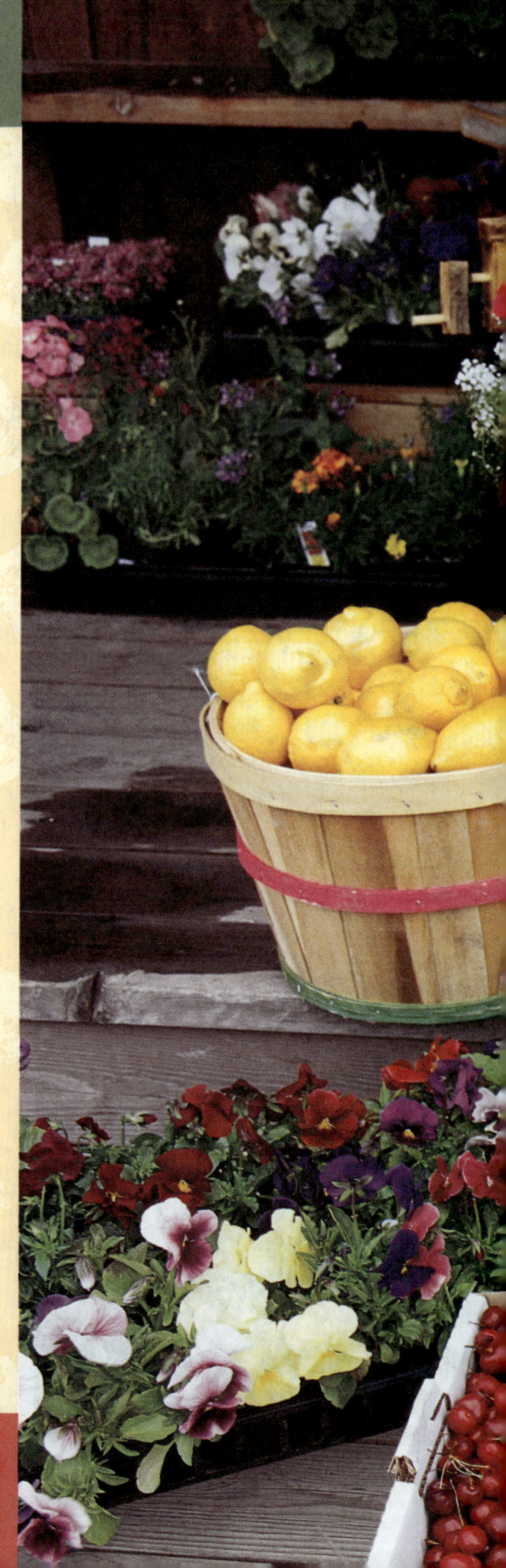

Baskets and boxes of summer's harvest tempt visitors to this country store in Sisters, Oregon. Photo by Dianne Dietrich Leis/Dietrich Photography.

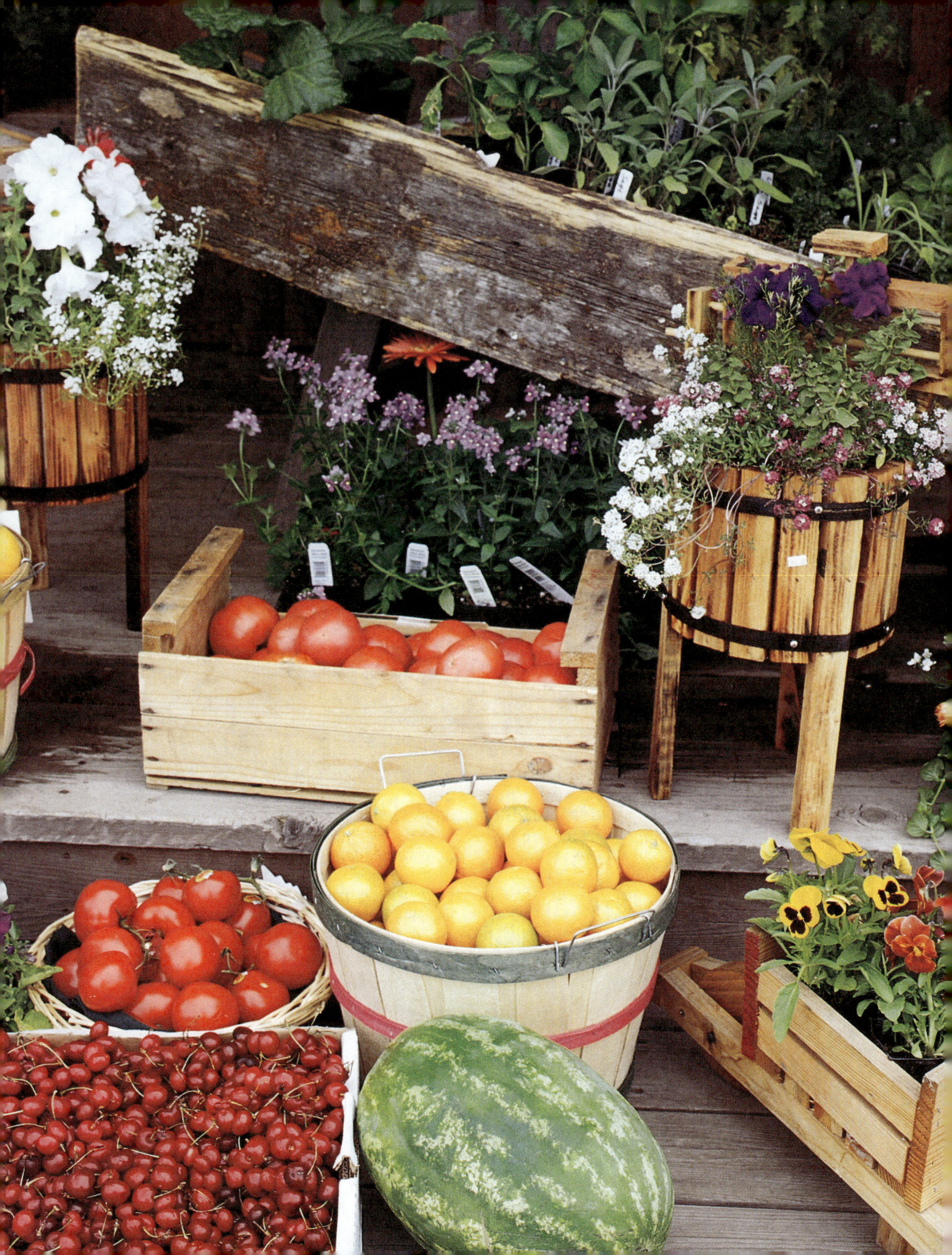

Of One Newly Come to America

Wilma Fritz Black

I saw the smoke curl up against the blue.
It was so early on that spring-bright day;
The orchard grass was silver-pale with dew;
Beneath the trees the scattered blossoms lay.

It drifted up beyond the maple trees.
I thought of her who laid the kindling spark.
Does she recall her home beyond the seas
And tremble now, remembering only dark?

Remembering only dark and fear and pain,
Does she look up with prayer to peaceful skies
And breathe her thankfulness for hope again,
So prayer and morning smoke together rise?

I do not know. But as I watched it rise,
I too thanked God for peaceful morning skies.

So at last I was going to America! Really, really going, at last! The boundaries burst. The arch of heaven soared. A million suns shone out for every star. The winds rushed in from outer space, roaring in my ears, "America! America!"

—Mary Antin

In Starlight, Indiana, a flag marks one farmer's pride in land and country. Photo by Daniel Dempster.

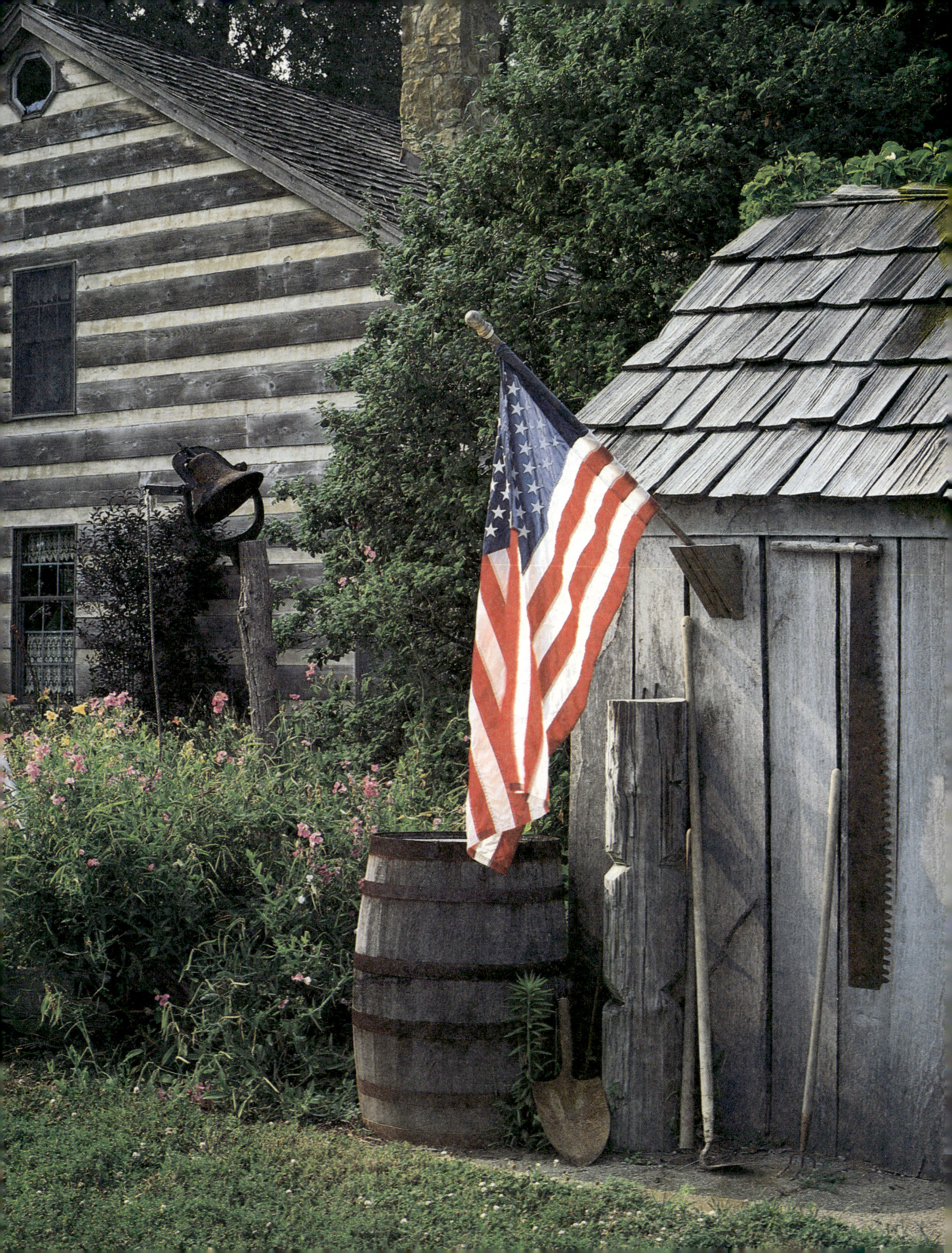

Prayer,
Thursday, July 3, 1947

Peter Marshall

God of our fathers, whose almighty hand hath made and preserved our nation, grant that our people may understand what it is they celebrate tomorrow.

May they remember how bitterly our freedom was won, the down payment that was made for it, the installments that have been made since this Republic was born, and the price that must yet be paid for our liberty.

May freedom be seen not as the right to do as we please but as the opportunity to please to do what is right.

May it ever be understood that our liberty is under God and can be found nowhere else.

May our faith be something that is not merely stamped upon our coins but expressed in our lives.

Let us, as a nation, not be afraid of standing alone for the rights of men, since we were born that way, as the only nation on earth that came into being "for the glory of God and the advancement of the Christian faith."

We know that we shall be true to the Pilgrim dream when we are true to the God they worshiped.

To the extent that America honors Thee, wilt Thou bless America, and keep her true as Thou hast kept her free, and make her good as Thou hast made her rich. Amen.

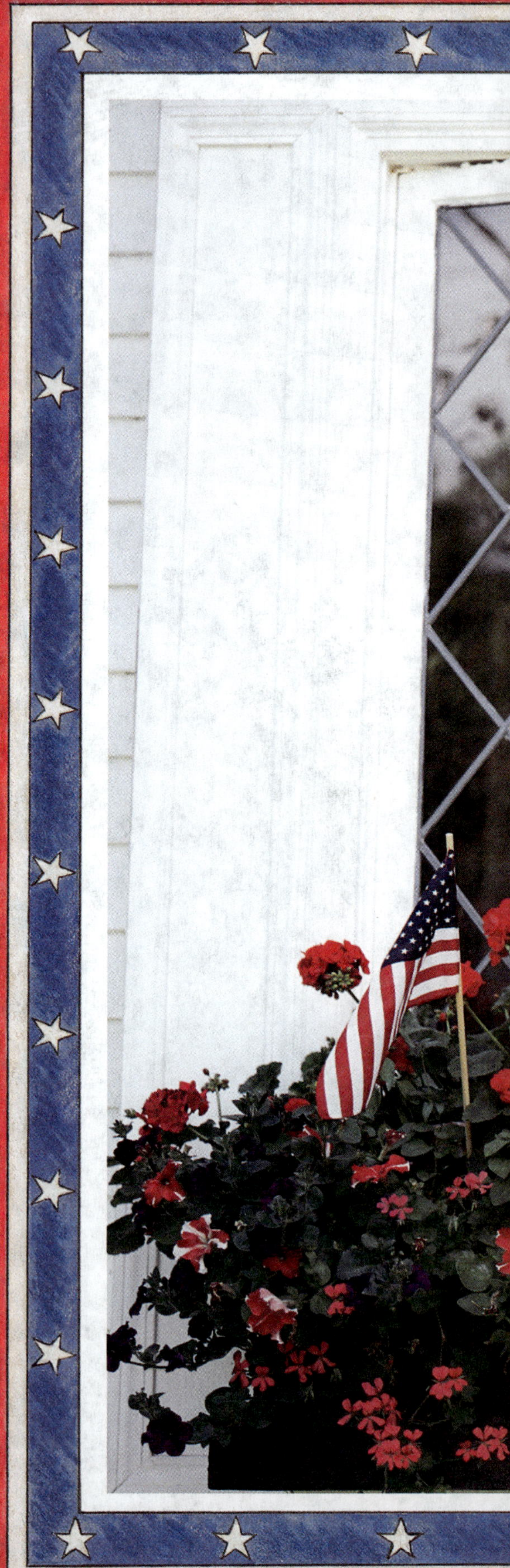

A profusion of flags and flowers bedecks a window for Independence Day. Photo by Dianne Dietrich Leis/Dietrich Photography.

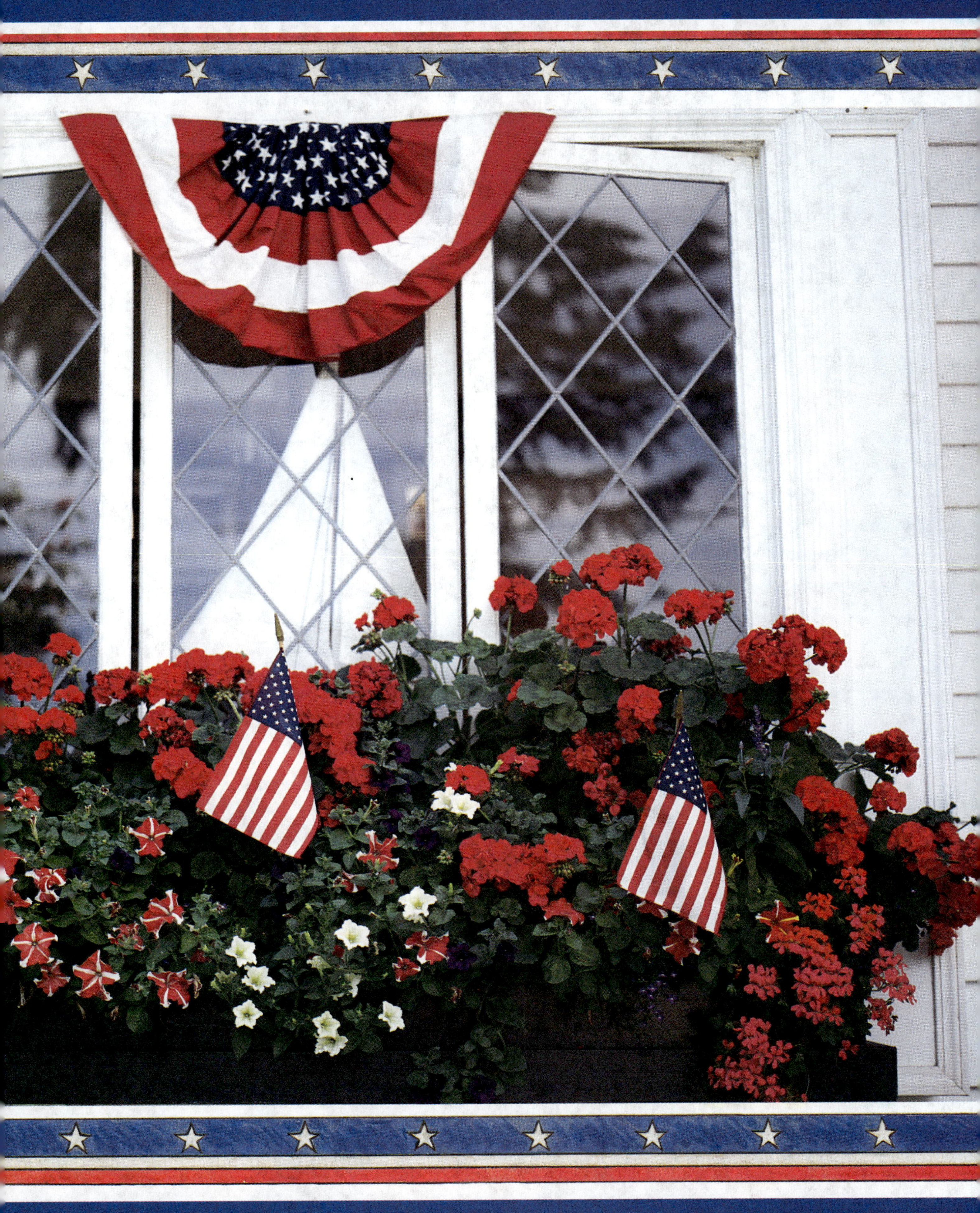

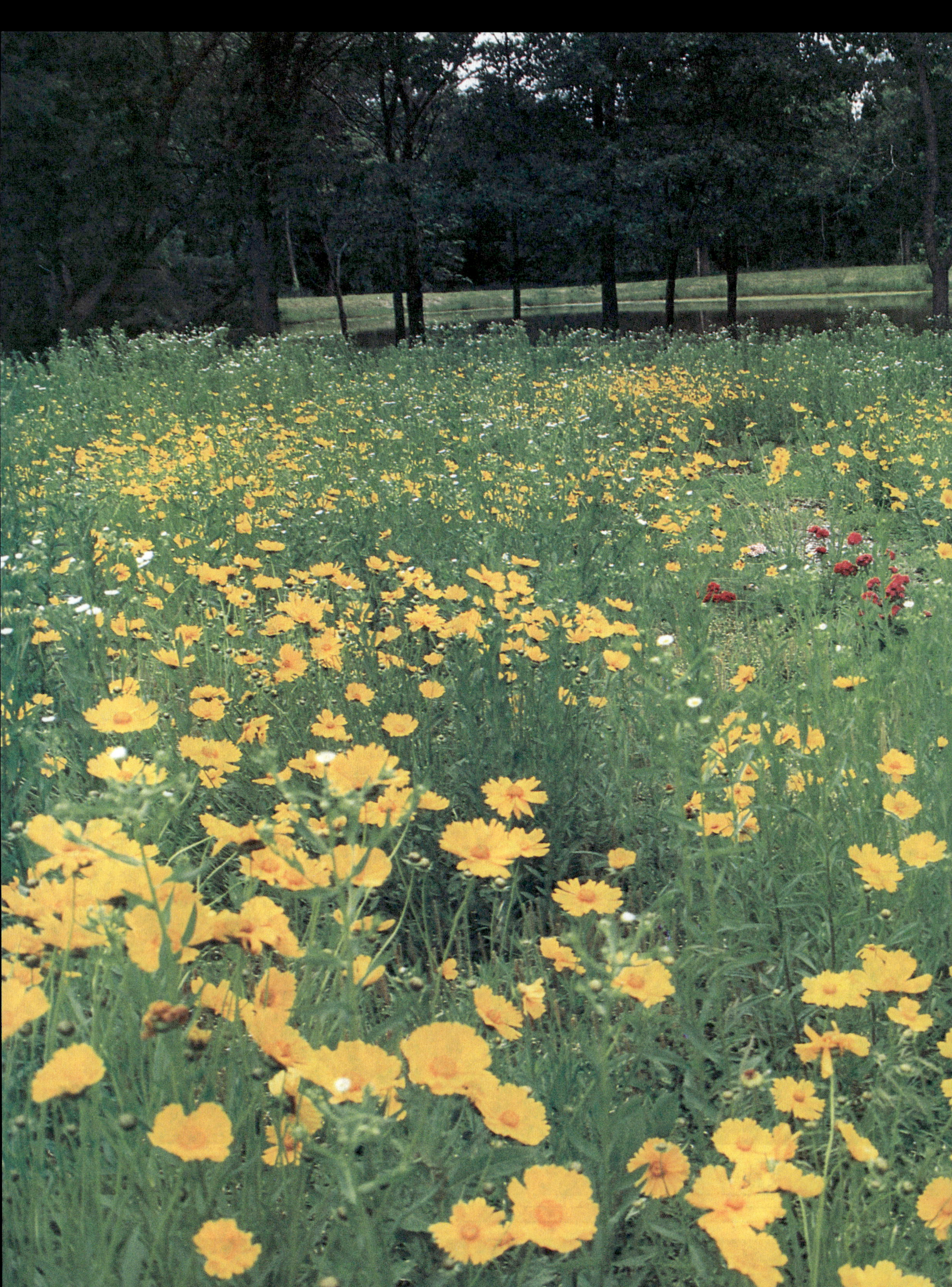

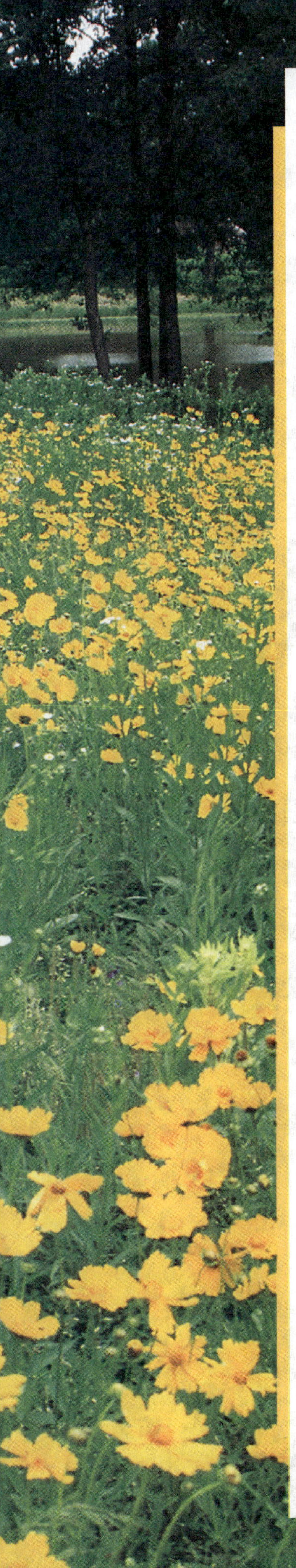

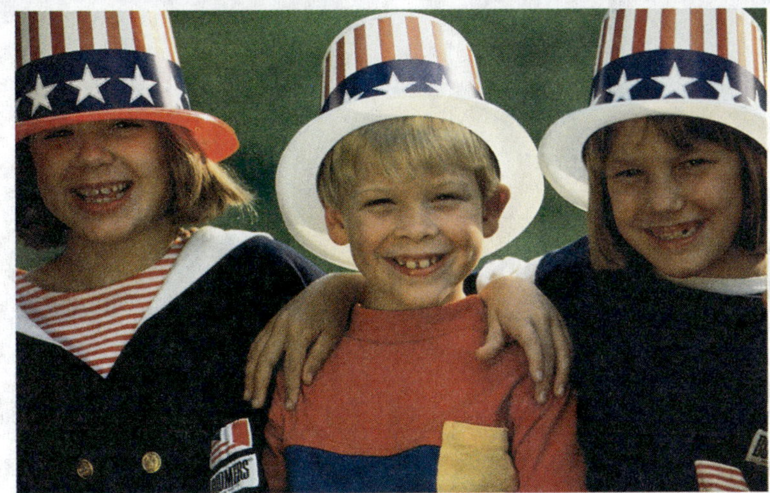

O Land of Mine

Charles L. H. Wagner

O land whose soul breathes liberty,
O land of hope where all are free,
Where children of each alien race
View not the tyrant's cruel face;
Where Pilgrims prayed and worshiped God
Without the fear of lash or rod
And left to us as legacy
The spirit of true liberty.

O land whose heroes of the past
Are with the world's immortals classed,
O land that gave us Washington,
Whose deeds have been surpassed by none,
O land which claims the resting place
Of Lincoln, saviour of a race;
Inspire me with their divine
And holy fire, O land of mine.

O land I love, when life shall cease
And my poor eyelids close in peace,
I trust that their last earthly view
Shall be the field of starry blue
And striped bars of red and white
Which fly triumphant for the right,
The glorious token and design
Of freedom's home, O land of mine.

Inset: Three young citizens celebrate their freedom. Photo by Bill Tucker/International Stock. Border: Wildflowers cover a field in Missouri. Photo by Gay Bumgarner.

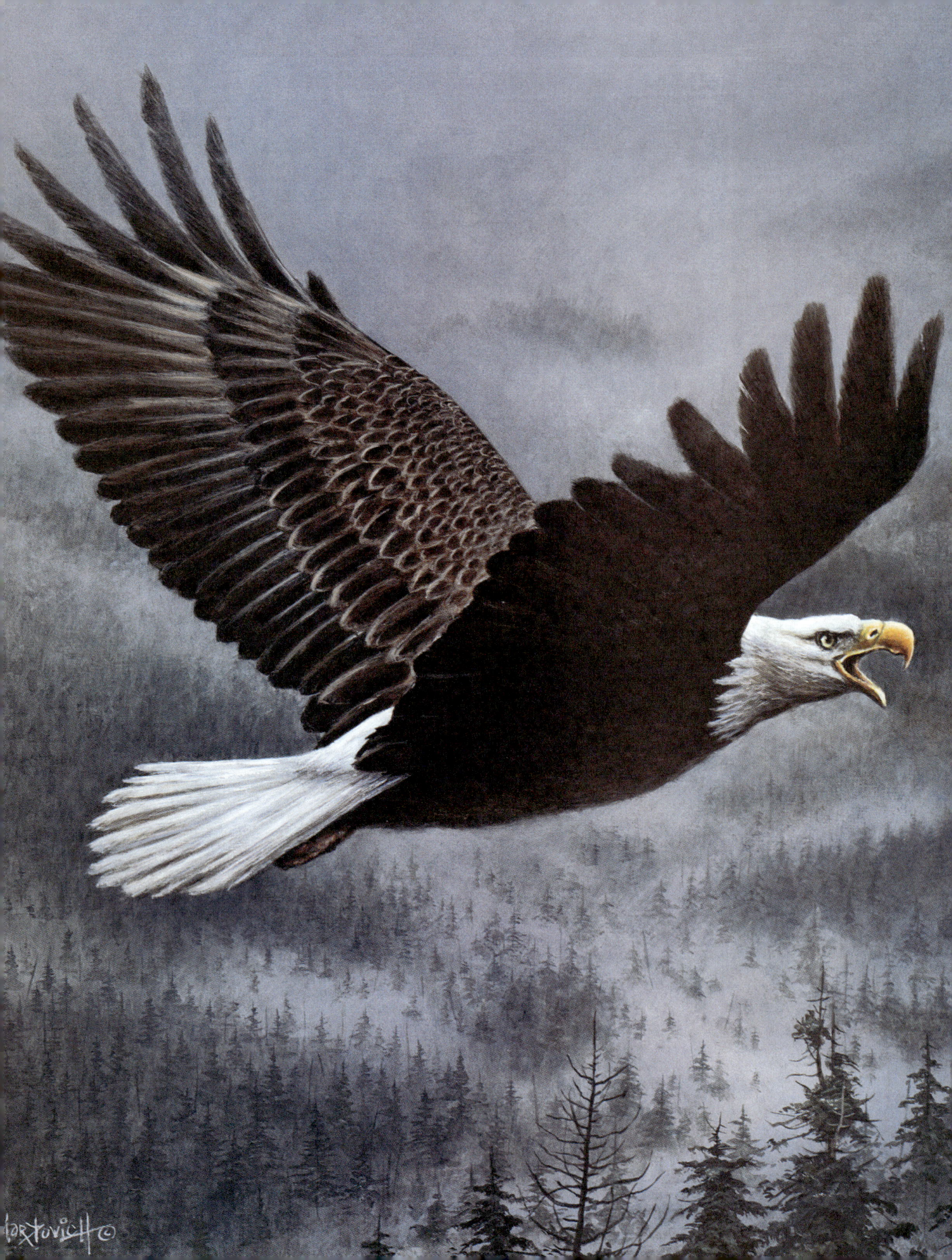

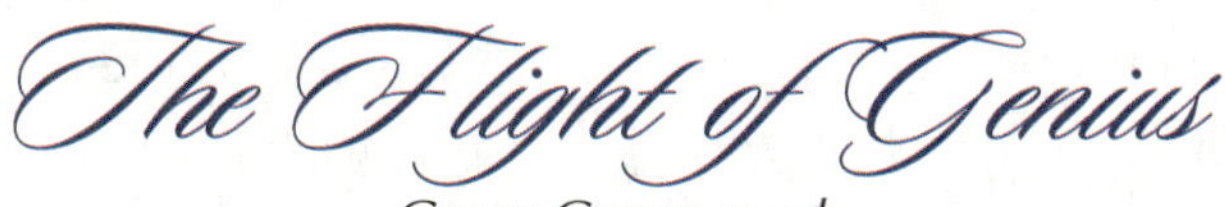

The Flight of Genius

Grace Greenwood

Where in their northern grandeur lie
Old Ocean's craggy shores,
Where waves give back the glorious sky
And lift unceasingly on high
Their deep, majestic symphony,
An eagle sunward soars!

Through upper air his flight doth ring,
And its portal-guarders frown;
They throng with angry muttering,
Their rattling ice-shot round him fling,
But he shakes the small hail from his wing
And royally soars on!

Yet a sterner, darker strife is nigh;
Wild storms come sweeping down.
Their thunders peal through the trembling sky;
Their red lights gleam on the quivering eye.
Small birds to their leafy coverts fly;
But the eagle still soars on!

Gaze high! For the thunder's realm o'erpast,
Now where warm glories spring,
Where no storm his way may overcast,
Outsoaring the lightning and the blast,
Lo, a golden cloud receives at last
The bird of the mighty wing!

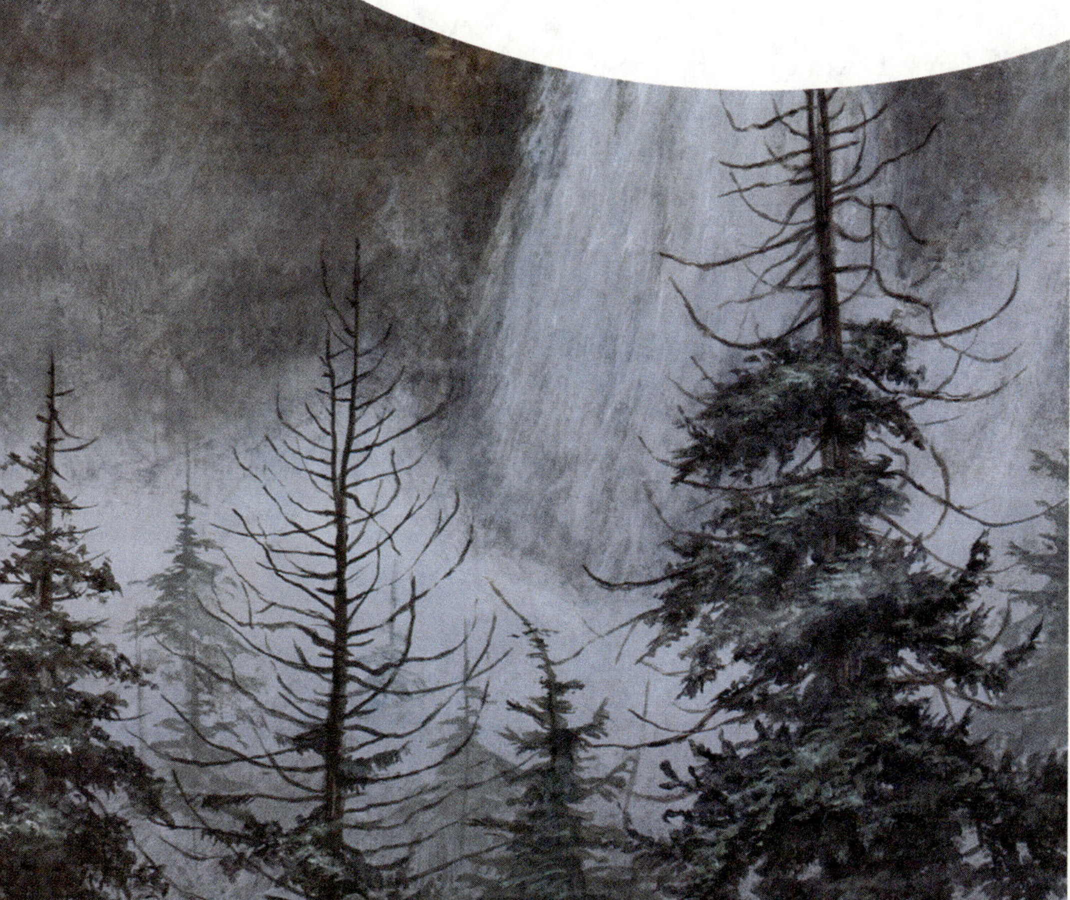

An eagle soars above the landscape in FREEDOM ON THE MIST *by artist Geof Markovich.*

Collector's Corner

American Eagle Memorabilia

Laurie Hunter

My cousin Joe has always been patriotic. Born on the Fourth of July, he never lets an Independence Day go by without organizing a neighborhood parade of some sort, even if it is only made up of his own kin.

Not surprisingly, when Joe was a boy, his birthday was celebrated with red, white, and blue decorations, spangled flags, sparklers, and striped stovepipe Uncle Sam hats. His gifts also reflected a patriotic theme. For Joe's first birthday, his mother had carefully perched a plastic bald eagle figurine, with wings outstretched, among the airy puffs of boiled white frosting on his cake. He was given a collection of American eagle postage stamps by his great-grandfather on his second birthday. By birthday number three, he had received a glowing American eagle night-light. It soon became apparent that a collection was hatching.

Through the years, Cousin Joe began buying up bits of America's glory for himself while patiently waiting for his next birthday. He hunted for Fourth-of-July postcards, matchbook covers, firecracker labels, jigsaw puzzles, and other odds and ends highlighting the American eagle.

Remarkably, Cousin Joe's American eagle collection has become a true reflection of himself and a concise snapshot of America's personality too—inspiring, patriotic, and resolutely passionate about freedom. Ranging from the rare to the everyday, from stiffly serious to whimsical, his discoveries include a coffee mug from the 1980 Olympic Games that bears a cartoon of "Sam the Eagle"; a set of hand-embroidered handkerchiefs sporting the nation's official eagle emblem; and a cast-iron mechanical bank dating from the early 1900s and shaped like Uncle Sam poised atop an eagle-decorated soapbox. Drinking glasses, snow globes, and plates spotlighting the illustrious bird fill his bookshelves. There is an eagle hand-carved by a World War I veteran. From the World War II era, Joe has a set of V-mail stationery bearing an eagle whose wings form a V for victory and a sterling silver pin adorned with rhinestone-encrusted eagle's wings. I also love his United States gold eagle coin, which is nine-tenths pure gold, dates from 1922, and was originally valued at ten dollars; who knows how much it would be worth today.

Joe can often be found rummaging through roadside flea market booths on the lookout for some under-appreciated American icon. From a dusty box, he scavenged a pair of brass lamp bases, each shaped like a proud eagle about to burst into flight. Once, at a garage sale, he found a milk glass candy container stained red, white, and blue in the shape of a little toy drum with an embossed eagle on the front; he bought it for twenty-five cents and discovered later it was worth almost one thousand times his investment.

Joe meticulously keeps track of each item in his collection: when it was purchased or from whom it was received, what had been its original purpose, what its former and current values are, and what he likes most about each item.

I wish I could remember exactly how many eagles are in Cousin Joe's collection; I know it must be nearly a hundred. I last saw him years ago at a family reunion. Some people brought their entire family with them. Others brought wallets spilling with accordion files of photos. Joe brought his American eagle collection, artfully arranged on several folding tables for all of the relatives to look at and enjoy throughout the weekend. Thumbing through one of the boxes filled with American eagle advertising and presidential buttons, I was glad to know someone who is so passionate about his hobby, so awe-inspired by freedom, and so proud to be an American. I can't look at Joe's collection of eagle memorabilia without being reminded of how precious this country really is.

An Eagle's Eye

As you begin scouting for American eagle memorabilia, the following information may be helpful.

History

• The Romans placed a golden eagle, their chief emblem, on the tip of a spear to represent strength, skill, and bravery. After the 1200s, the eagle became a favorite design on the shields of many knights and noblemen.

• The first eagle on an American coin appeared in 1776 on a Massachusetts penny. Since that time, the United States has made flags, coins, and paper money bearing the eagle.

• The bald eagle became the official emblem of the United States in 1787, when it was chosen over Benjamin Franklin's suggestion of a wild turkey.

• Due to a recent surge in nationalism, vintage coins, stamps, and other American eagle memorabilia have begun to surface on the collecting market. As people's consciousness of the value of patriotism has been raised, however, so has the price of antique patriotic items.

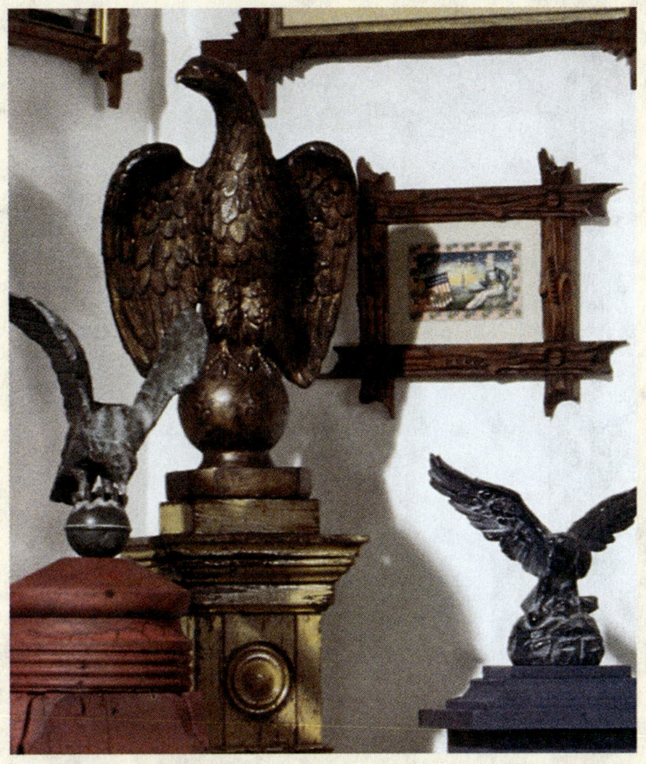

A patriotic collection spotlights a trio of eagles. Photo by Jessie Walker.

Getting Started

American eagles provide beginning collectors with a broad range of categories from which to narrow their search:

• Money, such as gold and silver American eagle coins
• Paper collectibles
• Works of art
• Statues or figurines
• Novelty items
• Patriotic souvenirs
• Advertising materials
• Lithographs
• Postage stamps
• Wildlife heritage memorabilia
• Collector's plates
• Coin jewelry (pendants, medallions, cuff links)
• Investor coin collections, such as the Coronet or Liberty Head Double Eagles—a rare collection of 150 coins that was minted between 1850 and 1907.

Tracking Eagles

• Both government-produced and commercially made goods bearing the American eagle are collectible.

• One-of-a-kind folk art figures of American eagles, particularly carefully hand-painted or antique items, make a collection unique.

• Affordable American eagle collectibles often include presidential buttons, posters, banners, World War I- and World War II-era advertisements and magazine covers, postcards, children's patriotic coloring and painting books, American souvenir spoons and mugs, and sheet music.

• Pricier collectibles include American eagle-shaped rarities such as iron doorstops, cookie jars, and weathervanes; vintage flags; antique coin and paper money; nineteenth-century trading cards; war uniform insignias and medals; and even salt and pepper sets, dinnerware, and bottle openers.

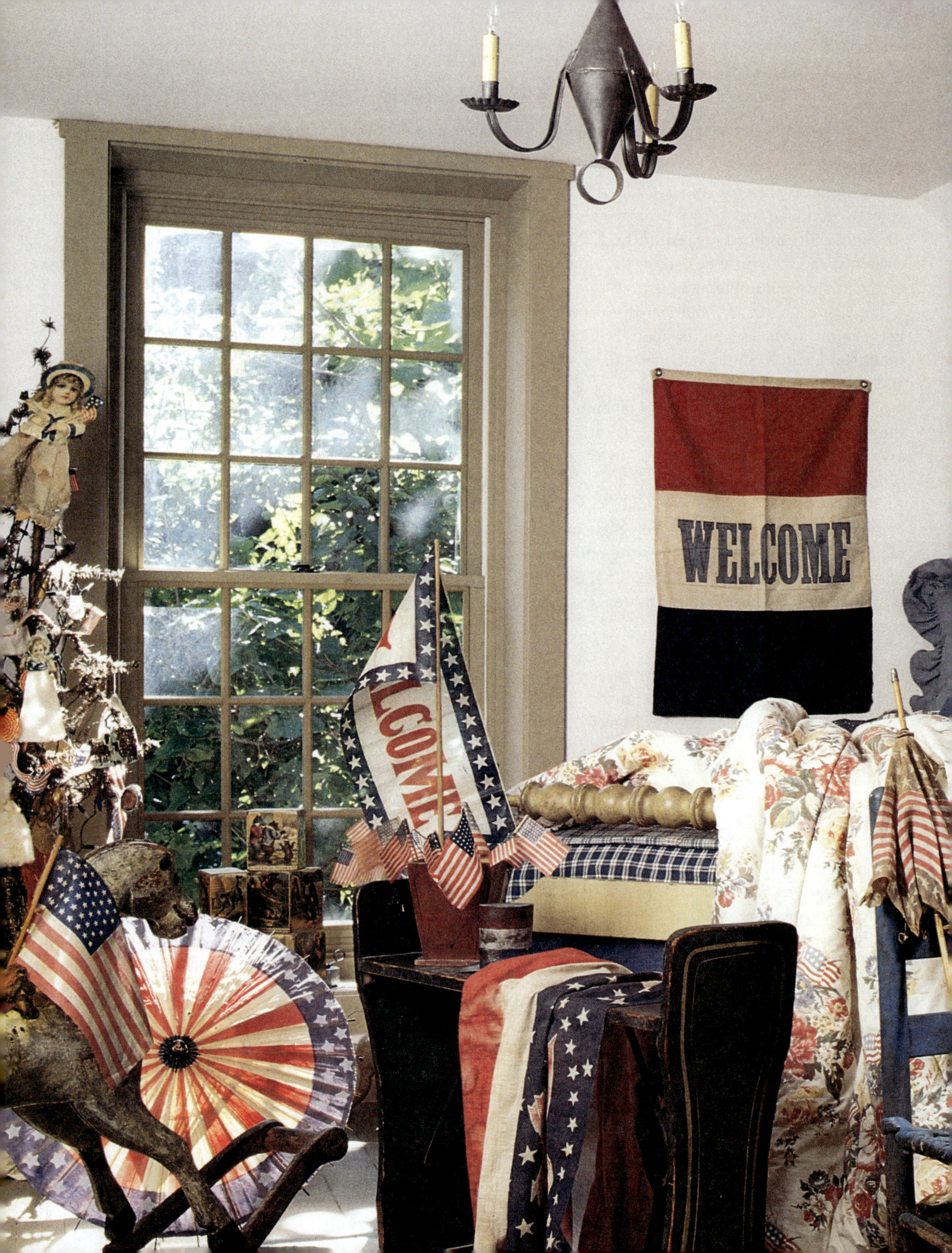
WELCOME
LCOME

Old Glory

Margaret Rorke

I'm just a bit of bunting dyed
In stripes of red and white.
My corner holds a field of blue
With stars to give it light.
Though winds may pull and tear at me
And sunny colors fade,
My spirit will remain as strong
As when I first was made.

My hist'ry is the hist'ry of
The land o'er which I fly.
Its freedom, pride, and power are
The things I signify.

I've been to all the battles that
My country's men have fought.
I've dwelt in all the school rooms where
The youngsters have been taught.

I watch you stand as I go by
With hat upon your heart.
You see in me a nation great
Of which you are a part.
Unfurled and floating on the breeze
In red and white and blue,
Your faith in home and fellow men
Is passing in review.

An attic room abounds with flags. Photo by Jessie Walker.

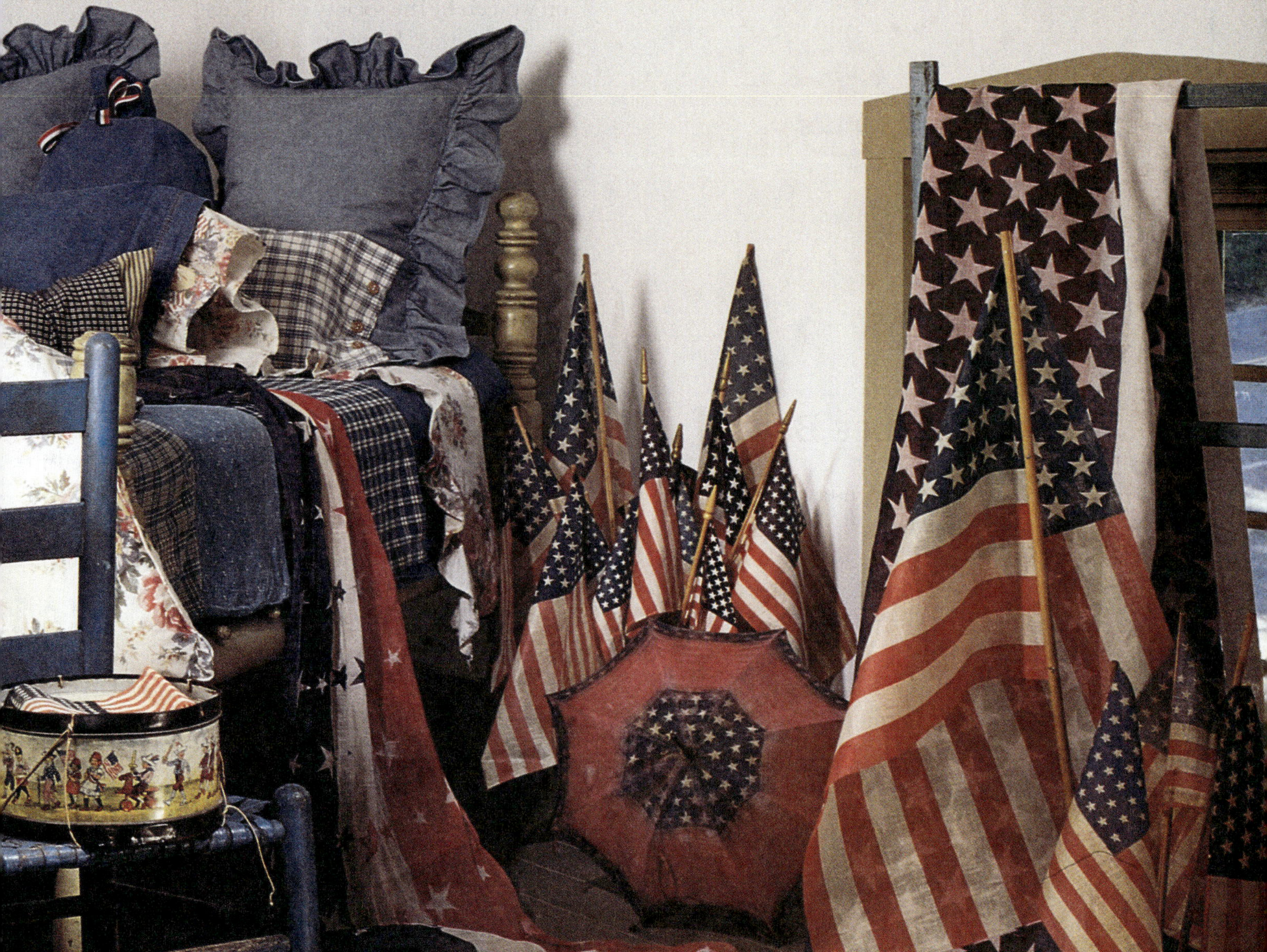

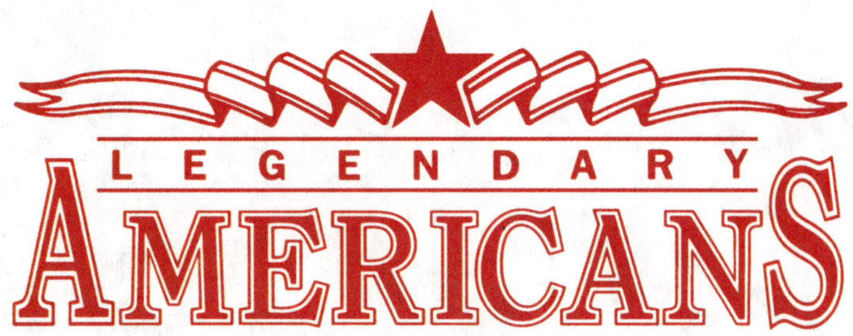

Nancy Skarmeas

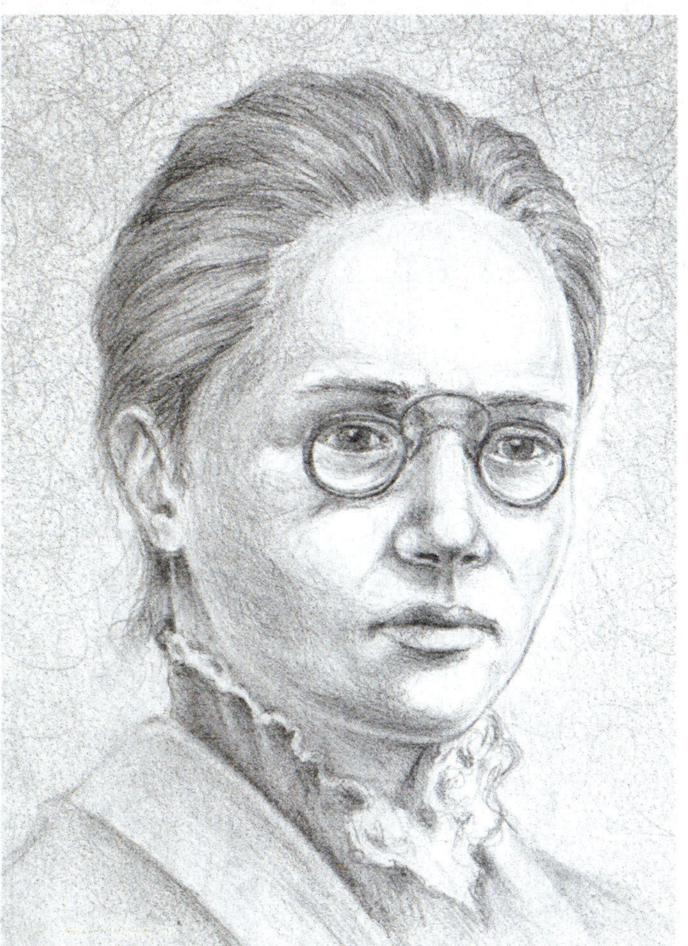

Katharine Lee Bates

Katharine Lee Bates, a conservative and unassuming woman who never sought the spotlight, likely would have been uncomfortable being called a "legendary American." Bates was intelligent and accomplished as a poet and a professor of English. She taught at Wellesley College for forty years and influenced the lives of countless young women who passed through her classes. She was a woman who quietly defied the conventions of her day to live an independent life of travel and learning. Yet despite Bates's influence and rich experiences, she turned away the praises and accolades heaped upon her. Nonetheless, nearly seventy-five years after her death, Bates retains the legendary status she earned one July day in 1893 when she stood atop Pikes Peak in Colorado, looked out upon the glorious American landscape that surrounded her, and wrote the lyrics to our beloved national song, "America the Beautiful."

Bates was thirty-three years old when she climbed Pikes Peak and penned the poem. She had brought with her to the mountaintop a thirst for knowledge and a lifelong love of poetry, both traits fostered since childhood by a family that, atypical of the time period, valued education for their daughters as well as their sons. Bates's mother was a graduate of Mount Holyoke Female Seminary, the first all-female institution of higher learning in the United States. Her grandfather had been president of Vermont's Middlebury College. Katie, as Bates was called by friends and family, lost her father just after her birth but was raised by a strong-minded mother who taught her daughter not to accept the educational limits placed on women by the society of their day.

Bates was born in Falmouth, Massachusetts. When she was twelve years old, her family moved to the small town of Grantville—now known as Wellesley Hills—just west of Boston. The move would prove quite fortuitous for the young Bates, because it put her in the neighborhood of a new experiment in female education called Wellesley College. When Bates was seventeen years old, she joined the second full class of students at Wellesley. At a time when only slightly more than ten thousand American women were enrolled in college, Bates flourished at Wellesley, especially in the areas of science, language, and literature. She wrote poetry prolifically and had the honor of seeing one of her poems published in *The Atlantic Monthly*. Bates graduated Wellesley in 1880 and went on to become a high school teacher. By 1885, however, Bates was back at her alma mater as a member of the English literature faculty.

Bates grew into a skilled and beloved instructor. Her passion for literature inspired great devotion and affection among her students. She continued to write daily, a habit she had begun as a young child, and spent her breaks from teaching traveling the world. Bates visited England, France, Scandinavia, Egypt, and Syria, among other places, but longed, most of all, to see the American West. When Colorado College wrote in 1893 and asked Bates to join their summer faculty, she needed no time to deliberate. She accepted the offer and decided to turn the trip into a grand tour of America.

Traveling by rail, Bates left Massachusetts and headed west. Her first stop was Niagara Falls, where she marveled at the wondrous spectacle of the falls. From there she went to Chicago, where she toured the World's Colombian Exposition. Organized to mark the four-hundred-year anniversary of Columbus's arrival in the New World, the Exposition was a showcase of invention, art, and ingenuity and featured everything from the world's first ferris wheel to such innovations as the zipper, carbonated soda, and picture postcards.

The mood at the Exposition was infectious. Bates left Chicago with a renewed sense of national pride and confidence. She arrived in Colorado Springs in July and settled in for three weeks of teaching. On July 22, she eagerly joined a group of visiting professors making a climb to the summit of Pikes Peak, whose presence loomed above the city. Pikes Peak is by no means the tallest mountain in the American West; but for Katharine Lee Bates, who was raised among the soft hills of southern New England, the very sight of the mountain moved her. Her group rode the first part of the way by covered wagon and then switched to mules. Many of the professors grew weary or ill with the altitude; but they continued on, unwilling to let this golden opportunity pass. At the summit, they were rewarded. To the east lay the vast expanse of the Great Plains; to the west rose the rugged and imposing Rocky Mountains. It was an awesome sight indeed; and Bates, as so often was the case in her life, felt moved to put pen to paper.

Her own words tell what happened next: "It was there, as I was looking out over the sea-like expanse of fertile country spreading away so far under the ample skies, that the opening lines of the hymn floated into my mind." The words she wrote that day would become the lyrics to "America the Beautiful."

After returning to Wellesley, Bates put the lyrics aside for a time but eventually had them published as a poem called "America" in a Boston church paper. From there, the poem quickly gained popularity. Bates revised the lyrics again and again, and the poem, set to music, began to appear in hymnals. Eventually, popular opinion settled upon a piece of music by Samuel Ward as the best pairing with Bates's words. In 1911, Bates did her final rewrite of the lyrics. Since that day the song has been a constant, unchanging part of the American patriotic canon.

Katharine Lee Bates went on to live many years after writing her most famous verses. She continued to teach at Wellesley, travel, and write poetry; but always and everywhere she was hailed and praised as the author of "America the Beautiful." Bates was thrilled to see her words so warmly embraced by the American people but was uncomfortable asserting ownership of her work. Her first five-dollar payment for publication of the poem was the only money she ever accepted; she freely allowed her poem to be published as long as the lyrics were unchanged. She called the poem "my own slight gift to my country."

Katharine Lee Bates retired from teaching at Wellesley in 1925 and died four years later. She had lived what was, in many respects, an unconventional life for her times. She was an independent, intellectual, working woman when such were uncommon in American life. She did not ever marry or bear children. In other ways, Katharine Lee Bates was a typical American of her era. She believed wholeheartedly in the beauty, the spirit, and the potential of the growing nation she proudly called home.

Throughout her life, Bates said that she considered herself not the creator of the lyrics to "America the Beautiful" but merely the scribe who put them to paper. Modesty aside, it was Bates who turned the pride and patriotism shared by countless Americans into the stirring and beautiful words we all cherish. It was she who gave voice to the soaring American spirit at the end of the nineteenth century and gave her nation a hymn for the ages. For this accomplishment, one outstanding moment in a life well and fully lived, Katharine Lee Bates will be forever a legendary American.

Nancy Skarmeas is a book editor and mother of two young children, who keep her and her husband quite busy at their home in New Hampshire. Her Greek and Irish ancestry has fostered a lifelong interest in research and history.

America the Beautiful

Katharine Lee Bates

O beautiful for spacious skies,
For amber waves of grain,
For purple mountain majesties
Above the fruited plain!
America! America!
God shed His grace on thee
And crown thy good with brotherhood
From sea to shining sea!

O beautiful for Pilgrim feet
Whose stern, impassioned stress
A thoroughfare for freedom beat
Across the wilderness!
America! America! God mend thine every flaw,
Confirm thy soul in self-control,
Thy liberty in law!

O beautiful for heroes proved
In liberating strife,
Who more than self their country loved
And mercy more than life!
America! America! May God thy gold refine,
Till all success be nobleness
And every grace divine!

O beautiful for patriot dream
That sees beyond the years
Thine alabaster cities gleam,
Undimmed by human tears!
America! America!
God shed His grace on thee
And crown thy good with brotherhood
From sea to shining sea!

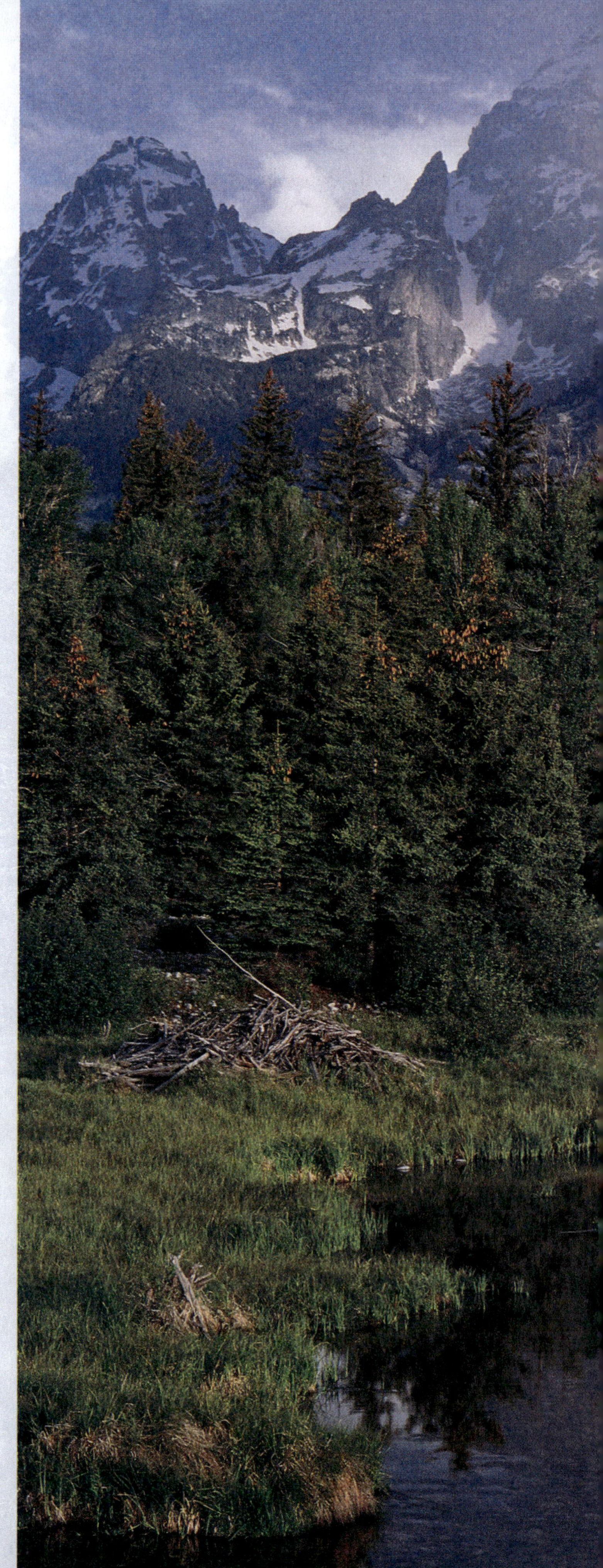

Purple mountains such as these in Wyoming's Teton Range prove America's majesty. Photo by Carr Clifton.

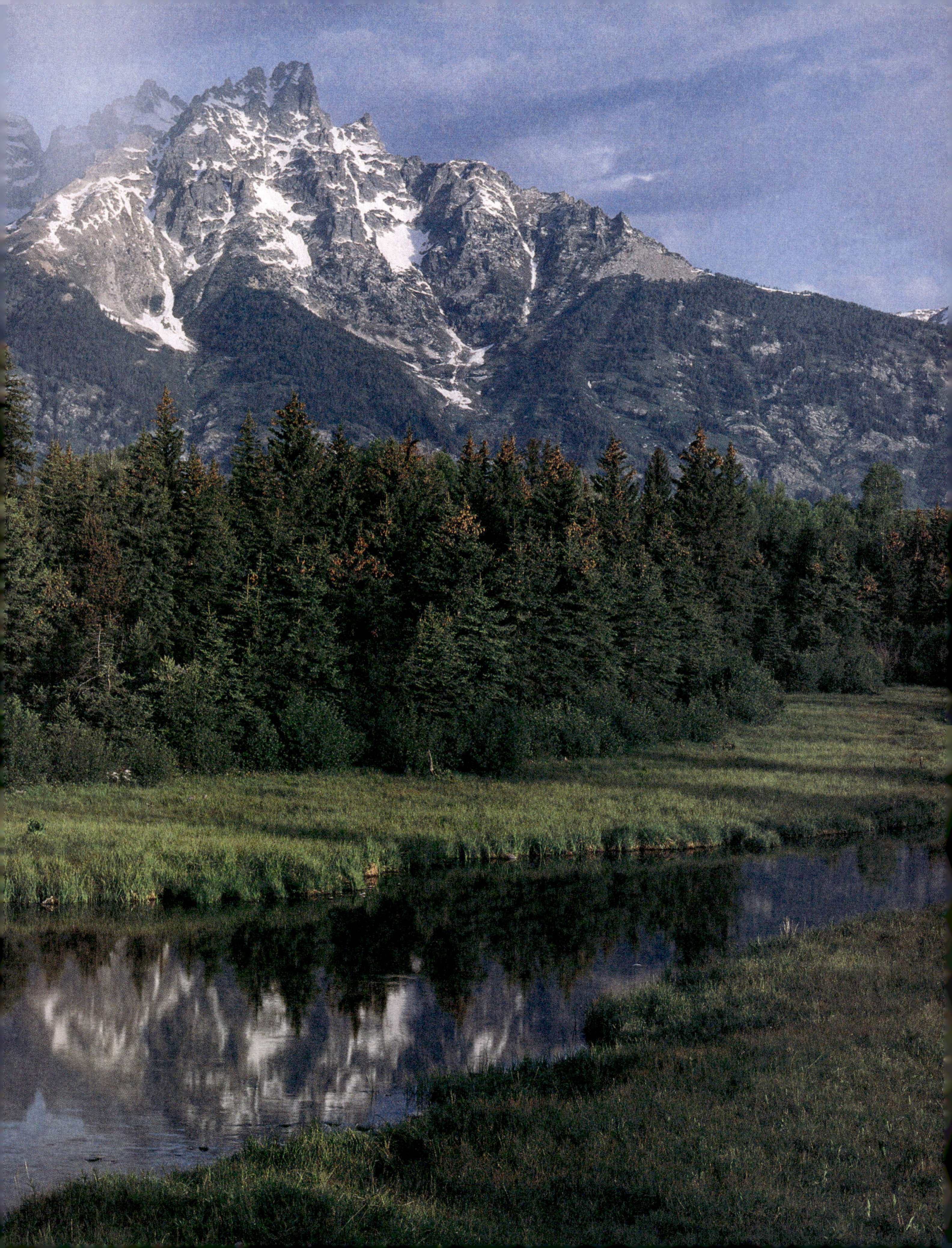

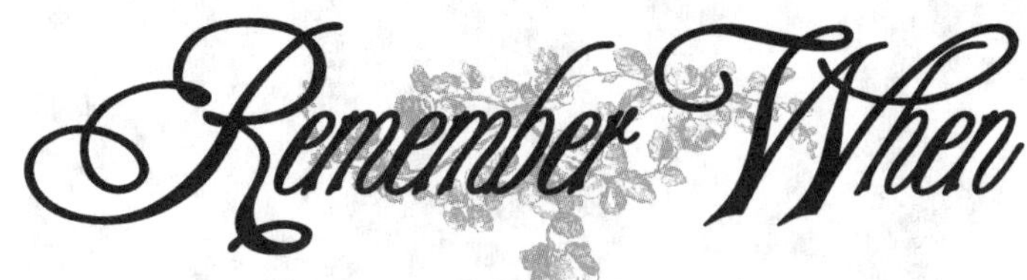

Quiet Town

Susan Allen Toth

It was a quiet town and a quiet time. That may be why I can still hear the whispers of notebooks slapping shut and a pencil sharpener grinding in the high-school study hall; the scratchy strains of "Blue Tango" on an overamplified record-player at the Friday dance; the persistent throb of grasshoppers in a rustling cornfield on a summer night. . . . In a world where nothing seemed to happen, small sounds were amplified so clearly that they still echo in my mind. So now on a hot summer night, when I sit by myself on my city steps, trying to block out nearby traffic and concentrating instead on the slightest rustle of leaves in the warm breeze, I remember the years of my growing up in Ames. Against that background of quiet, a girl could listen to her heart beating.

During the summer the long, hot weekend days seemed to stretch out like the endless asphalt ribbons of highway winding into the country. We never had quite enough to do, especially on Saturday mornings. When I plunge back into those uneventful Saturday mornings, I am once more lapped around by waves of time, repetitious, comforting, like the gentle undulations of Blaine's Pool when the late-afternoon breezes blew over its empty blue-green water. We all felt as though summer would go on forever. I would go to Olson's, or not; I would bowl a little, or not; I would see the boy I cared about, or I wouldn't. Other Saturday mornings stretched ahead like oases in the shimmering sun.

As I grew older, I began to realize that this quiet was not going to last. Time was speeding up; at some sharply definable point I would grow up and leave Ames. At odd moments in those last years I would be surprised by sadness, a strange feeling that perhaps I had missed something, that maybe life was going to pass me by. At the same time I nestled securely in the familiar landscape of streets whose every bump and jog I knew, of familiar people who smiled and greeted me by name wherever I went, of friends who appeared at every movie, store, or swimming pool.

Nowhere did I feel this conflicting sense of security and impending loss as sharply as I did at the train station. Ames lay on some important transcontinental routes, and trains passed through daily on their way from Chicago to Portland, San Francisco, Los Angeles. I had ridden on trains for short trips; but I had never been on one overnight, and I was too young to remember clearly what the country was like west of Ames when the prairies stopped and the mountains began. From a long auto trip when I was eight, I only remembered endless spaces punctuated by the Grand Canyon. So for me the crack passenger trains, the City of San Francisco, the City of Denver, the City of Los Angeles, had titles that ran in my imagination like the purest romance. Big cities, the golden West, life itself beckoned to me from every flashing train window.

On slow spring or summer nights I would often ask my friend Charlie to take me down to the station to watch the trains come in. The City of San Francisco was due to pass through at ten o'clock, the City of Denver at eleven. Down at the deserted station we sat on an abandoned luggage cart near the tracks and stared into the darkness, listening for the first telltale hoot of a faraway whistle. The night was so quiet that we whispered, hearing above our voices the grasshoppers, a squeal of brakes three blocks away, the loud click of the station clock. The trains were always late, but we were in no hurry.

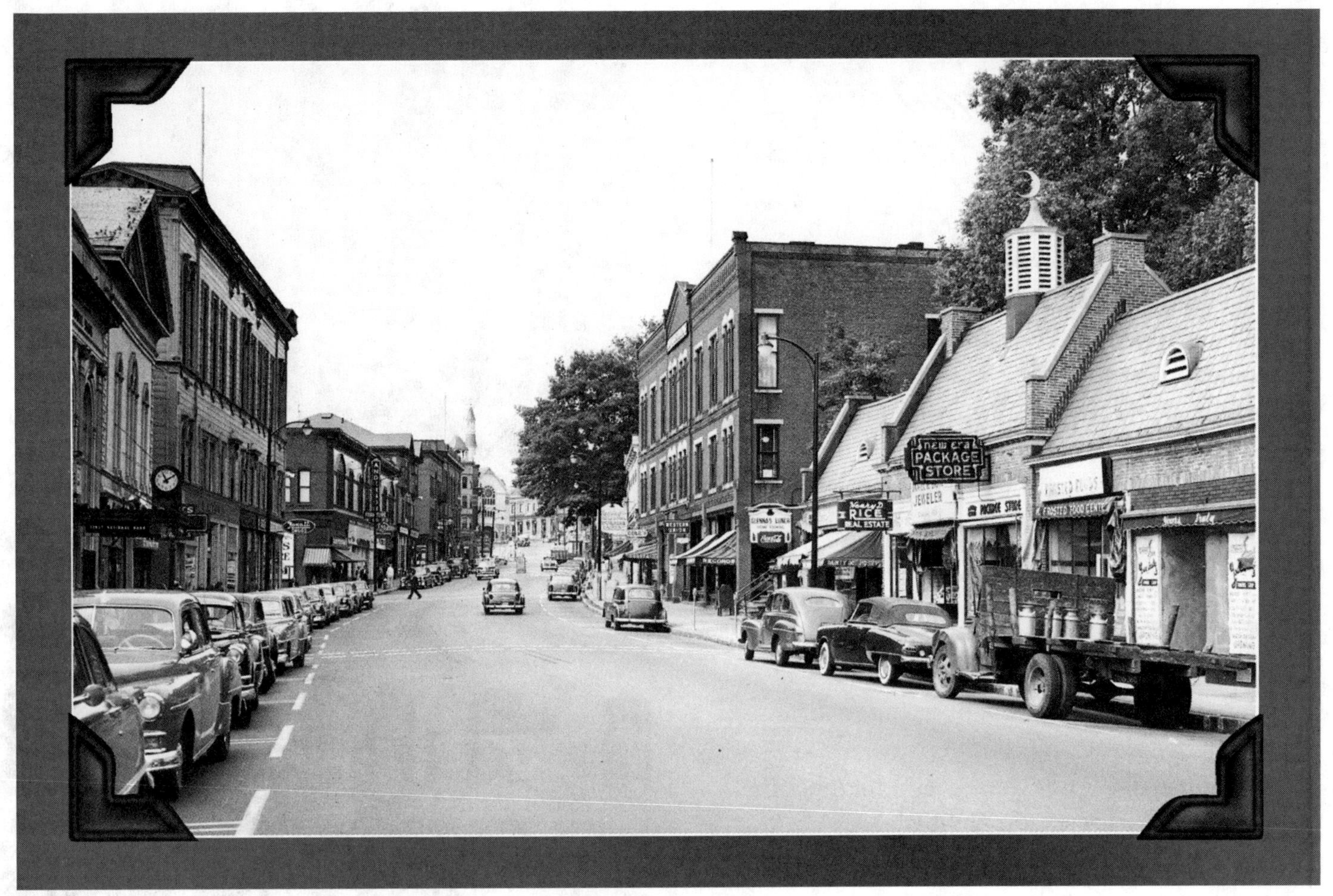

Main Street in Marlboro, Massachusetts, bears the familiar sights and sounds of yesteryear. Photo by Superstock.

Eventually we'd hear a rumble on the tracks and then see a searching eye of light bearing down on us. Quickly we'd leap to our feet and get as close to the tracks as we dared, plugging our ears as the train ground to a stop in front of us, its metallic clamor deafening, its cars looming in the night like visitors from another world. As we stood there, we could see people moving back and forth inside the lighted windows. If we were outside a Pullman car, we might catch a glimpse of someone seated next to the window staring wordlessly back at us. I wondered why everyone wasn't asleep. A frowsy-haired woman with a brown felt hat pinned to her graying curls looked like someone I might know but didn't. Two young boys, jumping on their seats and pounding silently on the glass, could have been the Evans kids down the street but weren't. They were strangers, separated from us not only by thick glass but by chance, being whisked away from their old lives to new ones. I felt the pull of the future, of adventure waiting for them and someday for me.

After a few moments, an exchange of luggage flung by the stationmaster who had suddenly emerged from inside the darkened hut, and a few shouts, the train began to grind again. As we winced with the jarring sound of metal against metal, it picked up speed. I tried to watch the car with the frowsy-haired woman and the two jumping boys, but it was soon lost in a blur of streaming silver metal. A last long, low shriek and the train was gone, off to Denver or San Francisco.

I always felt let down when Charlie and I walked back to his car. I comforted myself with thinking that someday I too would be traveling on one of those trains, leaving Ames for college someplace far away, maybe even Denver or San Francisco. When I got on that train, I would head into a new and wonderful life. It never occurred to me that I would be taking my old self, and Ames, with me.

Hometown

Daniel Whitehead Hicky

The town that I am proud to call my own
Is not a lighted city with towers of stone,
Nor a seaport sensuous with the smell of ships.
Yet when the day goes by and darkness slips
Into the hedges and the orchards there,
Of all the world I think my town most fair,
With lamps like casual fireflies in the dark,
And lovely as the singing of a lark
The children's voices and the crickets' choir
Lifting toward heaven as the moon rises higher.
My town lies seldom on a map or chart,
Yet bright it twinkles in memory of the heart.
And there I turn, a tired, forgotten man
Deep in the city's blinding, hurrying span,
To claim my peace, my lost identity
Where even the sunflowers' eyes remember me.

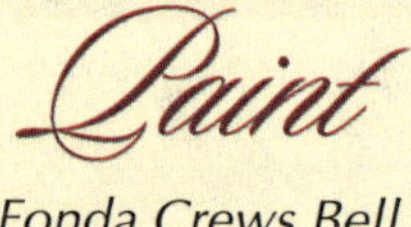

Fonda Crews Bell

Paint me a cardinal
Sitting in a pine.
Paint me a field
Of yellow-topped corn.
Paint me a church,
White against the blue.
And paint good folks around it
Walking two by two.
Add some streets and little stores,
All arched by heaven's dome.
Then paint me right on Main Street
And call me home.

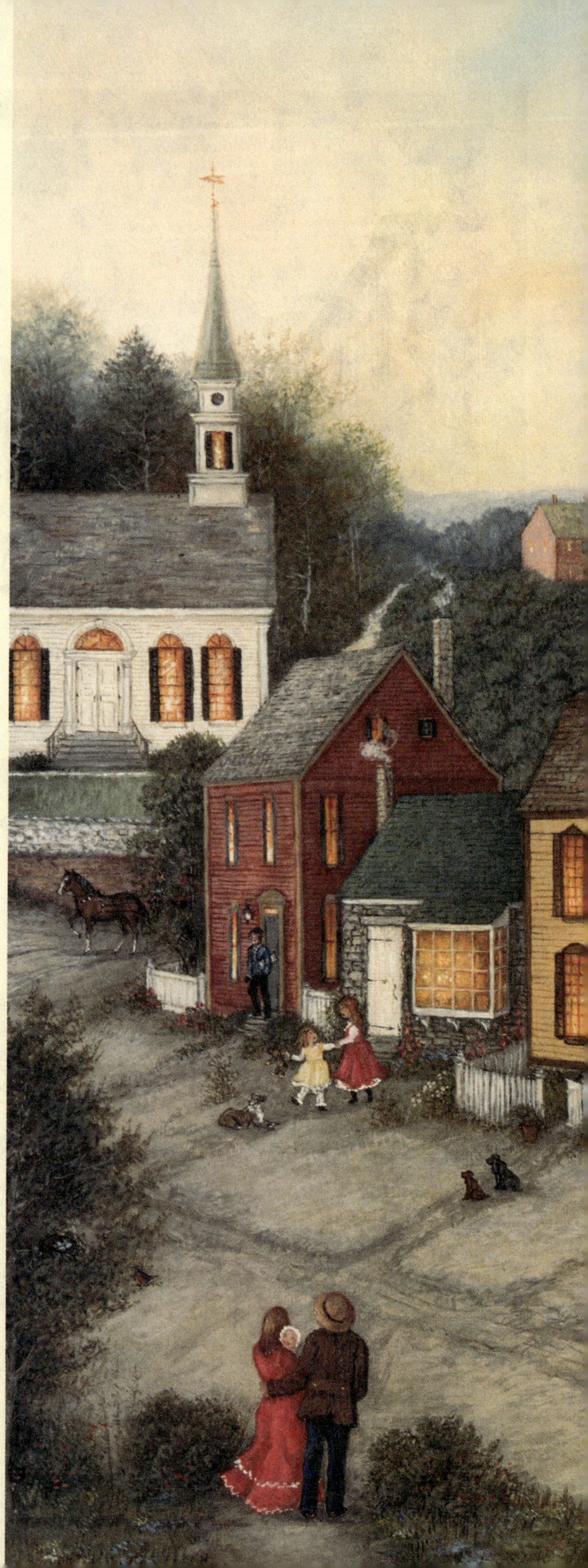

Townspeople head homeward in VILLAGE AFTERNOON *by artist Linda Nelson Stocks.*

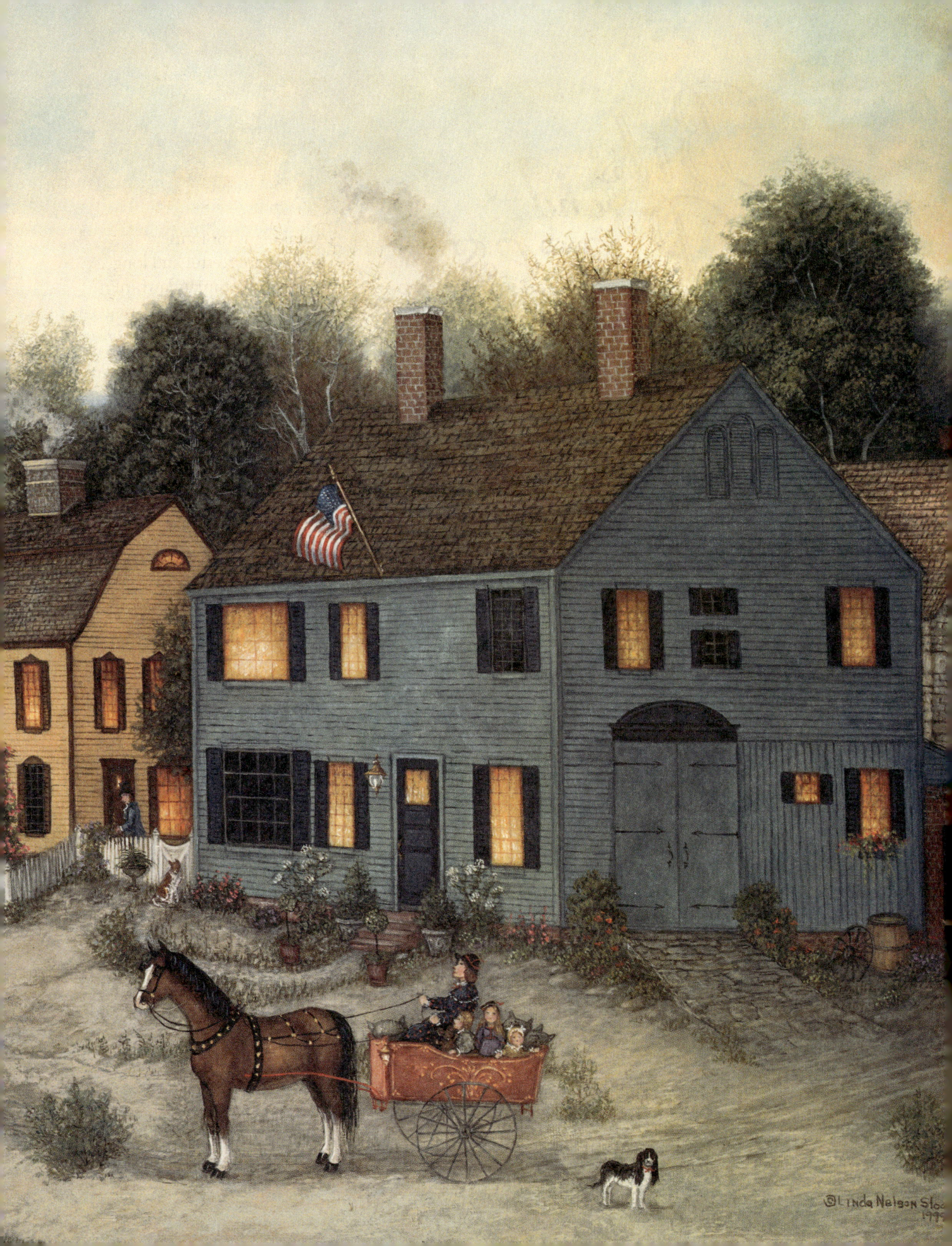

Bits and Pieces

Rural life is for living;
The days are zestful and long.
You greet the sun at dawning,
And the day begins with song.

—*Eleanor Fiock*

How blessed is he who leads a country life,
Unvexed with anxious cares and void of strife.

—*John Dryden*

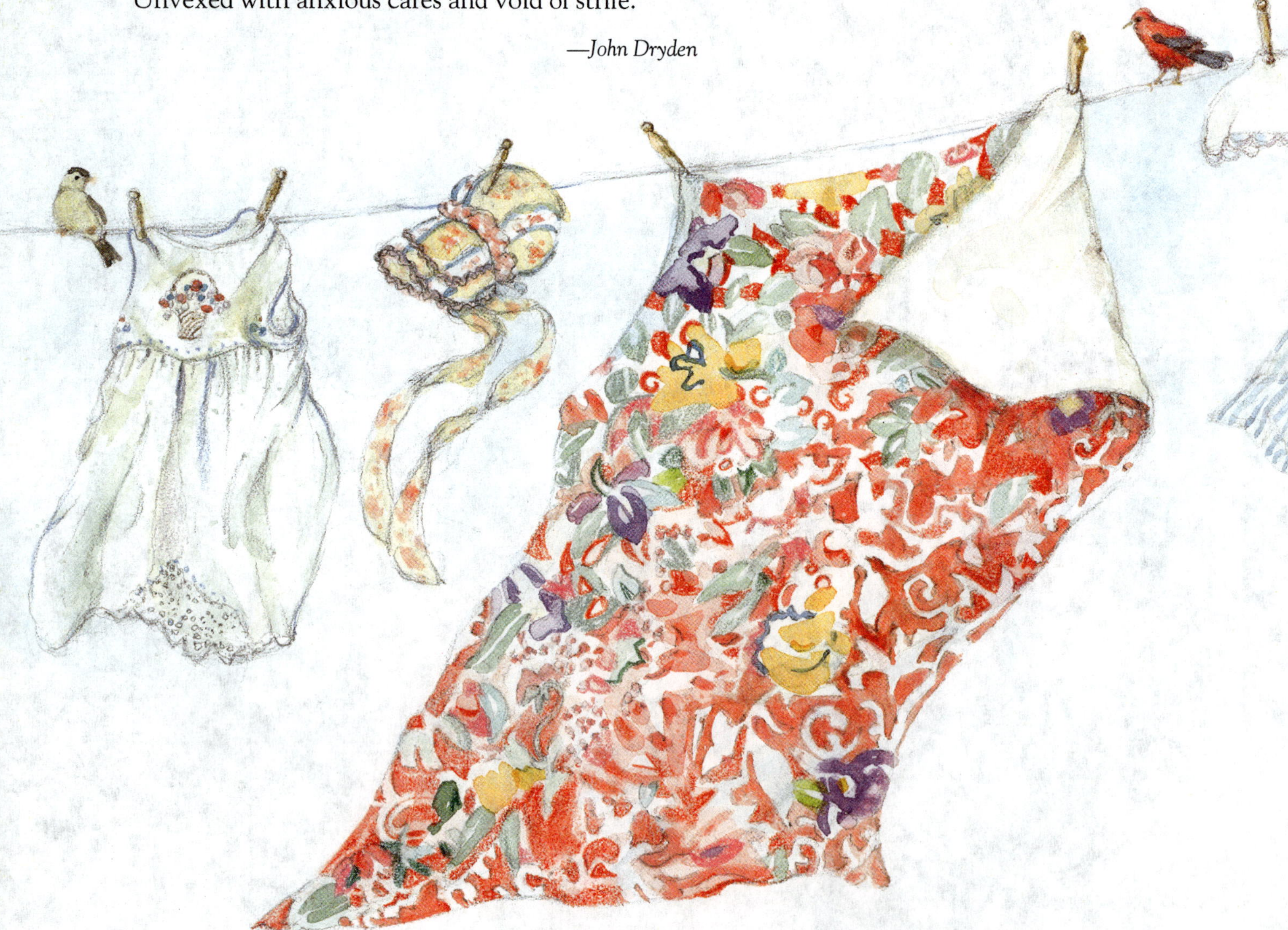

Men are taught virtue and a love of independence by living in the country.

—*Menander*

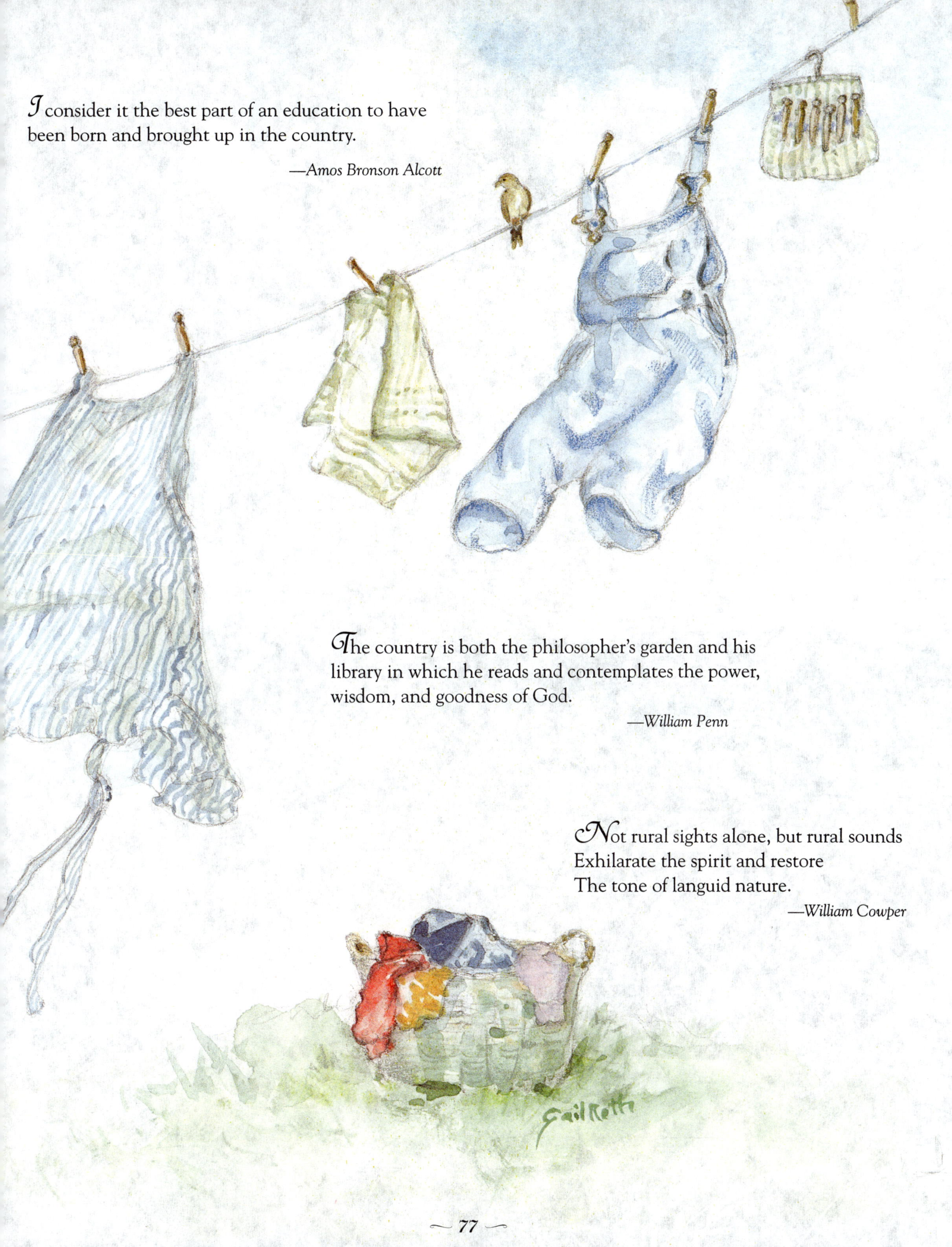

I consider it the best part of an education to have been born and brought up in the country.

—Amos Bronson Alcott

*T*he country is both the philosopher's garden and his library in which he reads and contemplates the power, wisdom, and goodness of God.

—William Penn

*N*ot rural sights alone, but rural sounds
Exhilarate the spirit and restore
The tone of languid nature.

—William Cowper

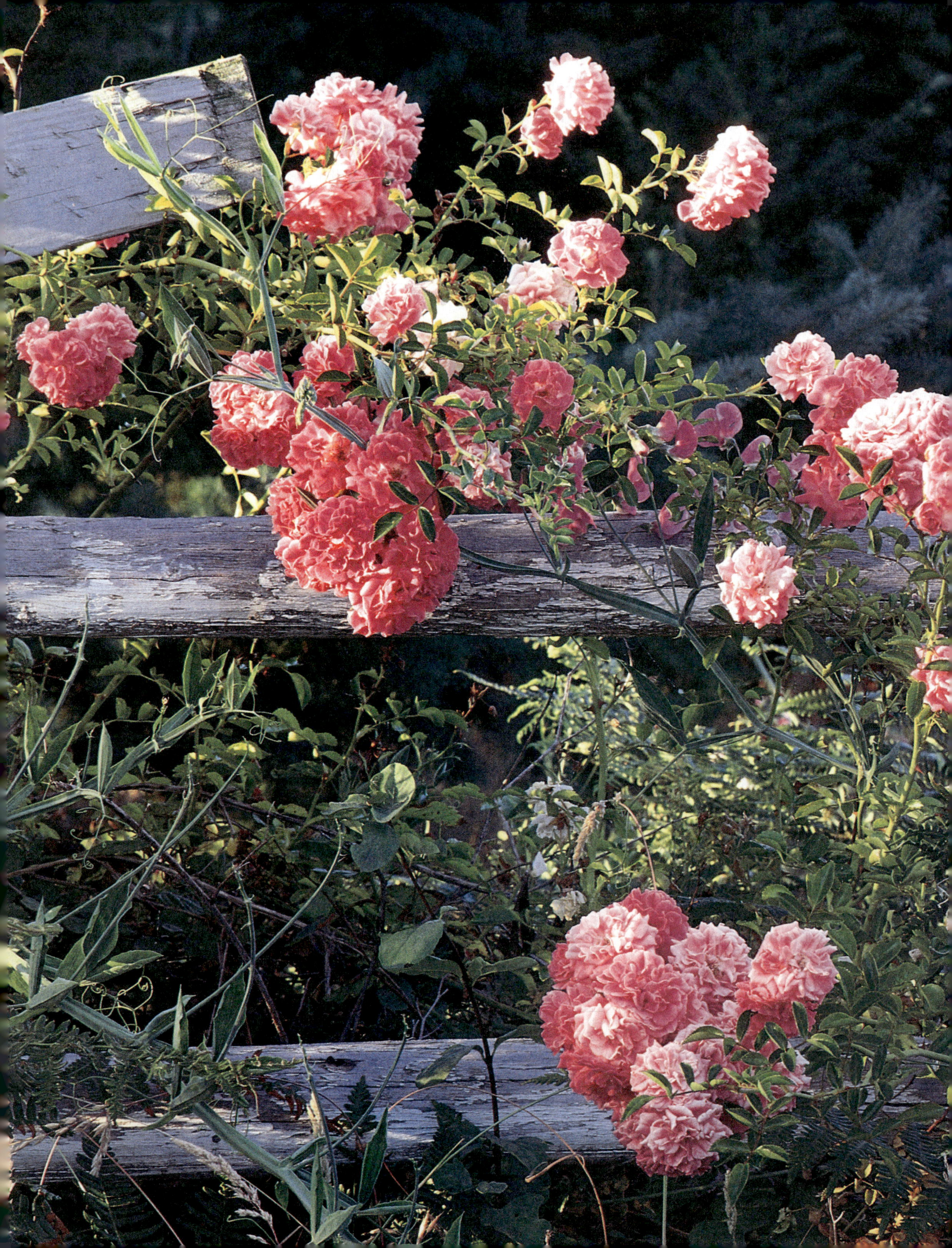

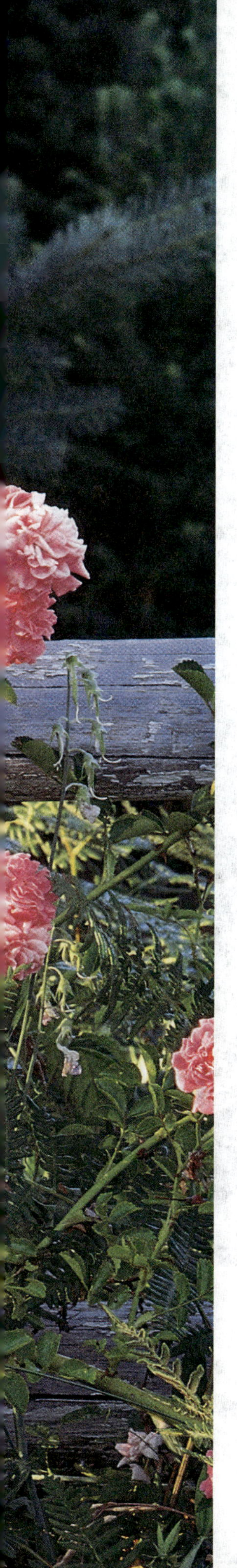

Country CHRONICLE

Lansing Christman

THE WILD ROSE

The other afternoon as I was driving along some country roads, I was delighted all along the way by the enchanting blossoms of roses climbing the road banks and spreading their reds and pinks among the vines and bushes, the grasses and weeds. My memory slipped back to the wild rose that thrived in the pasture across the creek from my old homestead. It has been thirty years since I saw the pasture, and I wonder if the rose is still there.

Miles away from these foothills of the Blue Ridge, I know that pasture as well as I know the seasons. Year-round it was open to me like the pages of a book. I was familiar with each page and with each flowing chapter. Morning after morning in summer, and again in the afternoon, I walked into that pasture to bring in the cows at milking time. I went in the freshness of the dawn and again in the serenity of late afternoon. I always brought back with me far more than the Holsteins. There were the birdsongs, both those of dawn and those of the later day. There were the aromas of the new-mown hay in the meadow beyond the stone wall and of the mints and evergreens and wildflowers. And always, there was the beauty and scent of the pasture's wild rose.

The memories have endured, though the pasture, with its thin-soiled, stony ledge, has long since reverted to its natural state. It has been planted to trees, not by man, but by nature. I wonder if the wild rose on that stony slope still finds enough sun to come into bloom when summer returns to the hills of home.

The author of three books, Lansing Christman has contributed to Ideals *for almost thirty years. Mr. Christman has also been published in several American, foreign, and braille anthologies. He lives in rural South Carolina.*

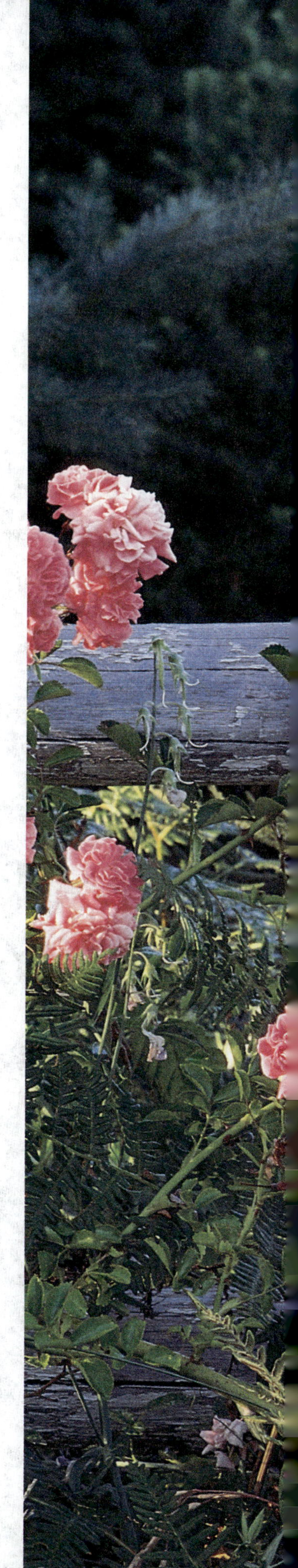

Wild roses tumble along a rustic fence near Alpine, Oregon. Photo by Dennis Frates.

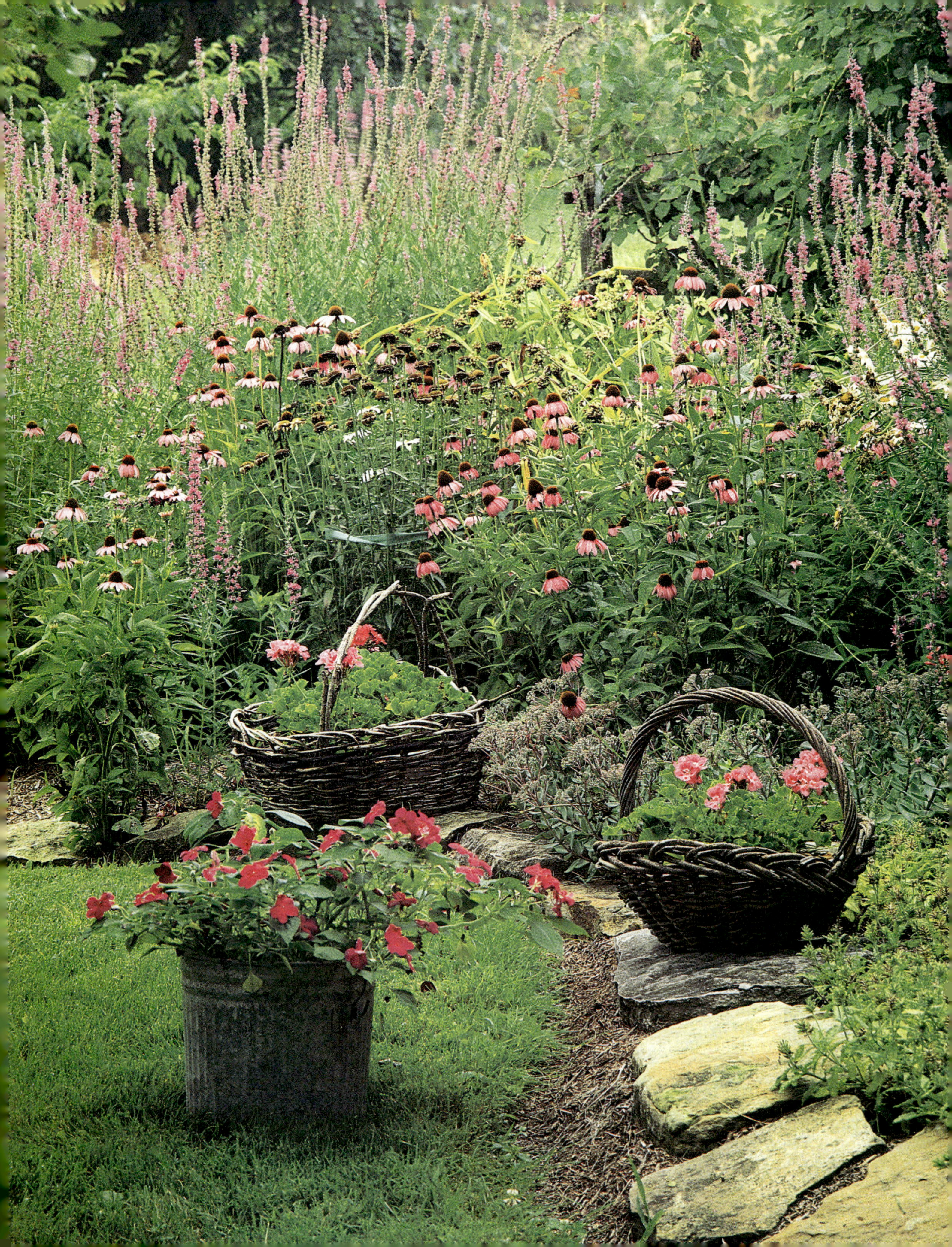

Artistry

Harold A. Schulz

Glad summertime is graced with artistry
Of flowers in multi-rhythmed tracery
Like fragile balls of white and purple phlox
And blushing faces of tall hollyhocks,
Long spears of foxglove reaching high,
And meadow daisies laughing at the sky,
Bright flares of asters, charming and sedate,
And shy petunias by the garden gate,
Red roses throwing perfume to the breeze
While honeysuckle caters to the bees.
The morning glories waken with the sun,
And four-o'clocks tell when the day is done.
These are the strokes of life and hope, the lines
Glad summertime artistically designs.

Treasures

Thelma J. Compton

I am no miser,
But I hoard the heap of summer's treasures
To count upon when winter winds sweep round each corner.
The daisies and the gold of buttercups
From emerald meadows;
The silver of raindrops and brooks lit by summer suns;
The diamonds of uncounted dewdrops
Sparkling the early mornings;
The pearl of clouds set in sapphire blue
And opals of a sunset sky;
Rubies in red roses;
Amber of a woodland stream;
Topaz of a sunrise;
These are mine, and rich am I.

A country garden in Greenville, Indiana, holds summer's treasures. Photo by Daniel Dempster.

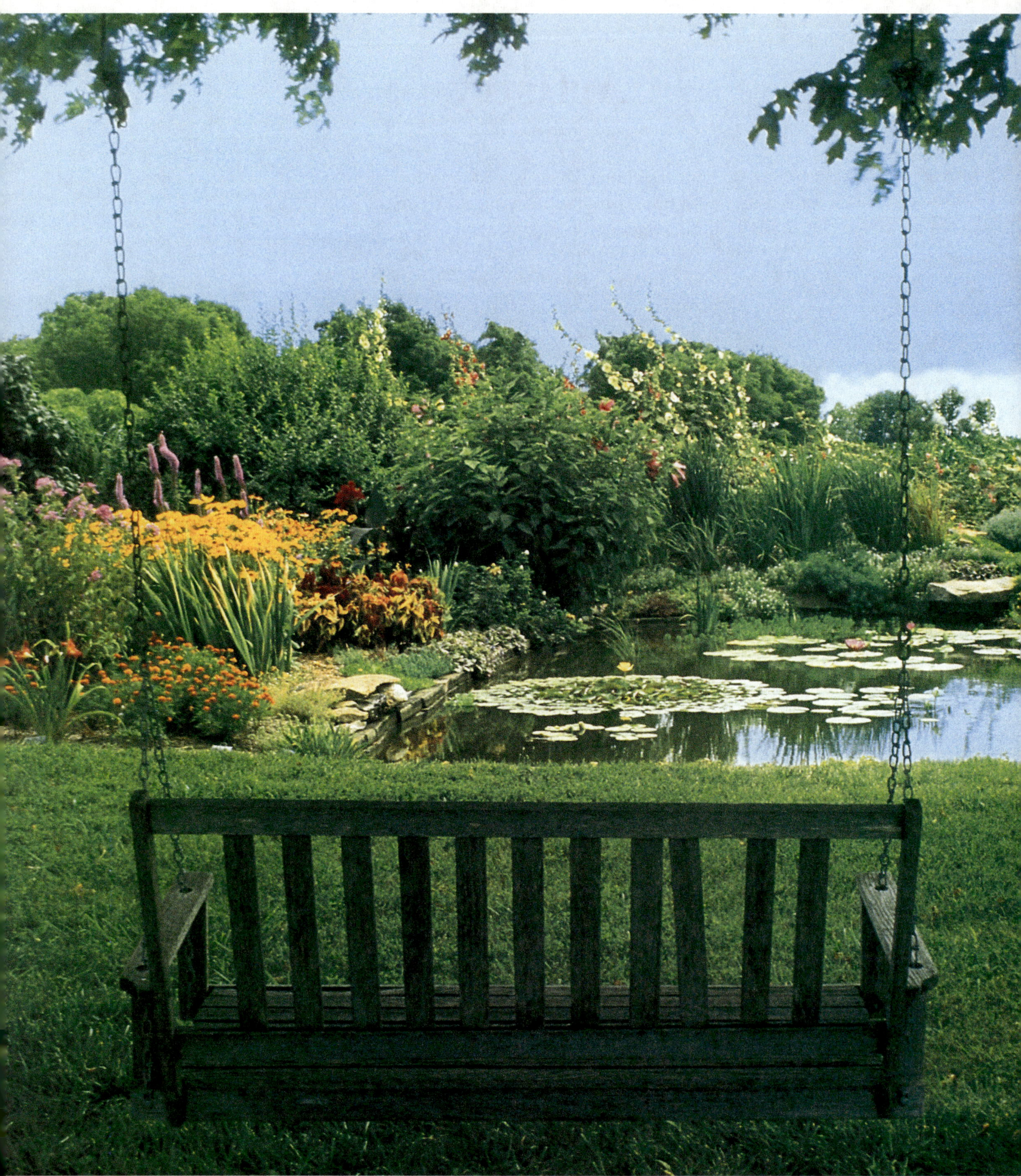

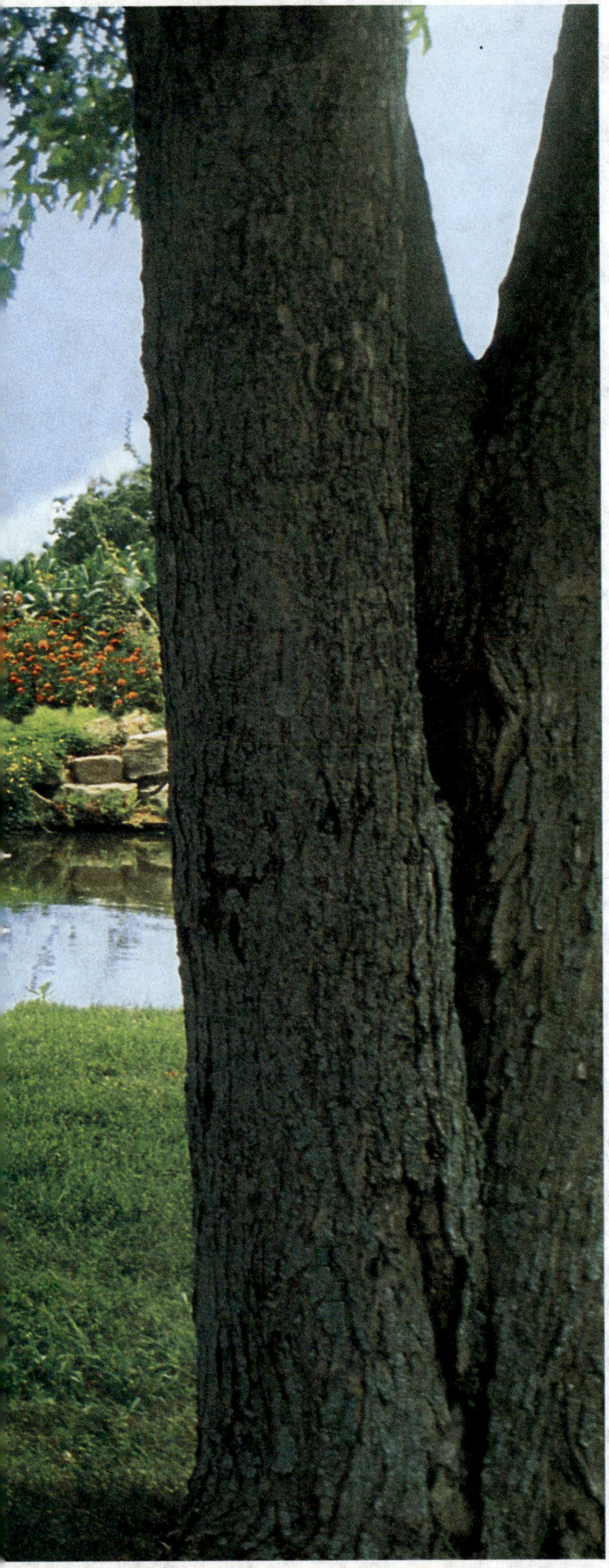

Madame Croesus

Maidee L. Boyd Smith

Because I have a mirrored pool
The jeweled stars are mine;
The birds give all their songs to me
From the choir loft of my pine.

The sun heaps gold about my feet
In poppy coins, new-minted bright,
And down my garden path the moon
Glows silver-cool and white.

Shining Things

Grace V. Watkins

How wonderful that there should be
Such lovely, shining things:
A hillside maple, autumn-bright,
A meadow pool reflecting light,
An oriole on skyward wings,
A small allegro brook that sings,
And hearts to feel a rhapsody
Of joy that we can hear and see!

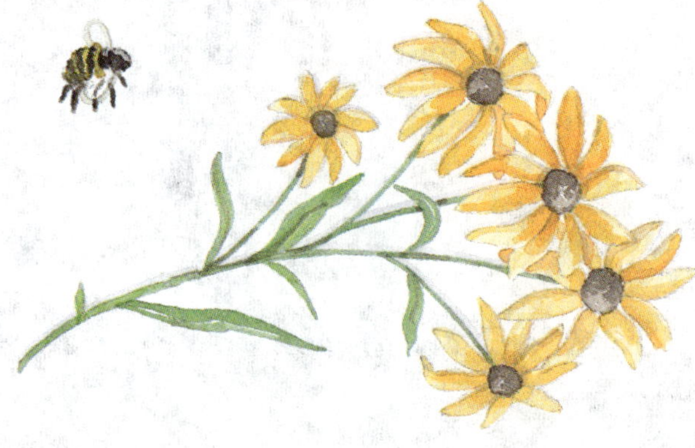

A swing captures a view of a mirrored pool in Missouri. Photo by Gay Bumgarner.

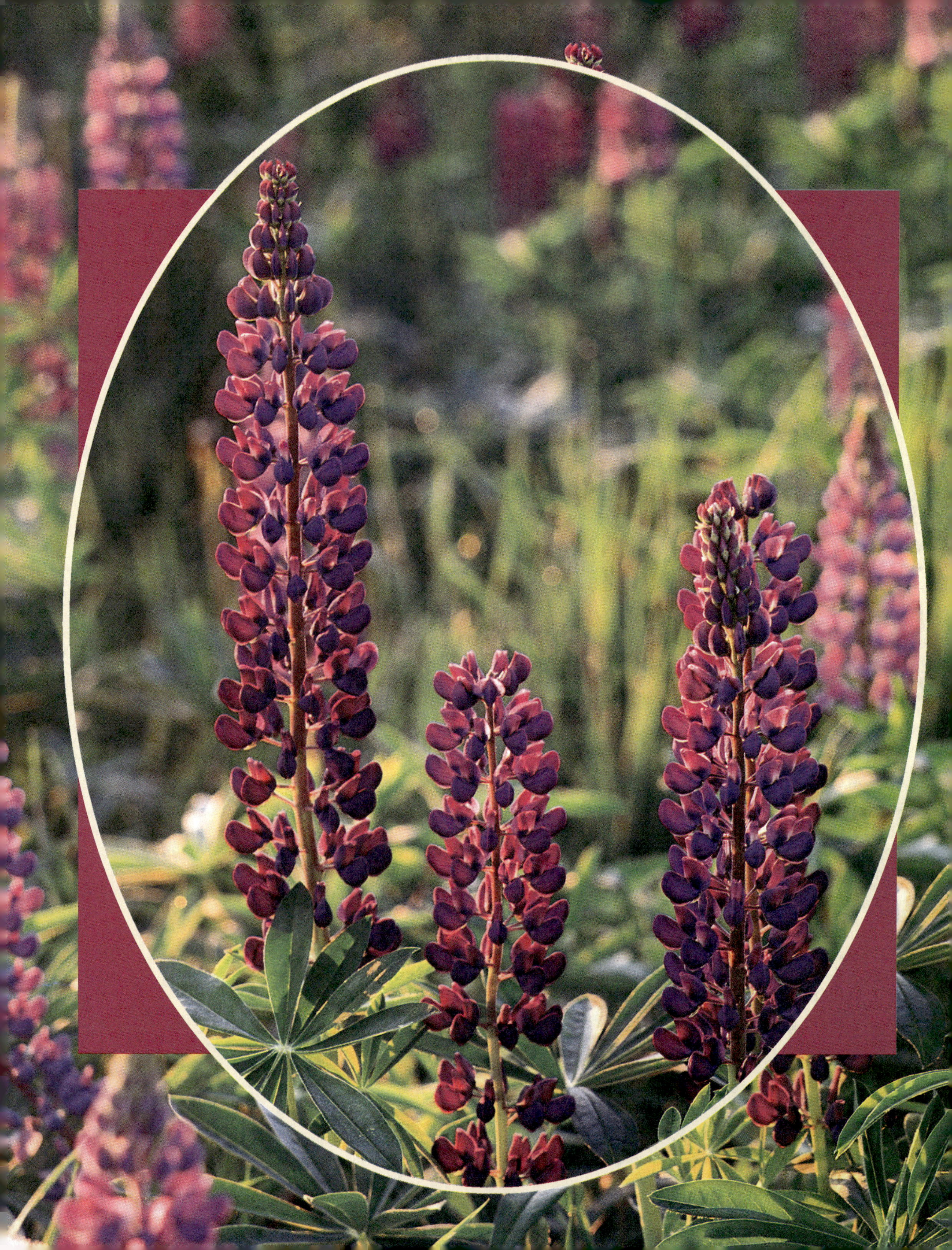

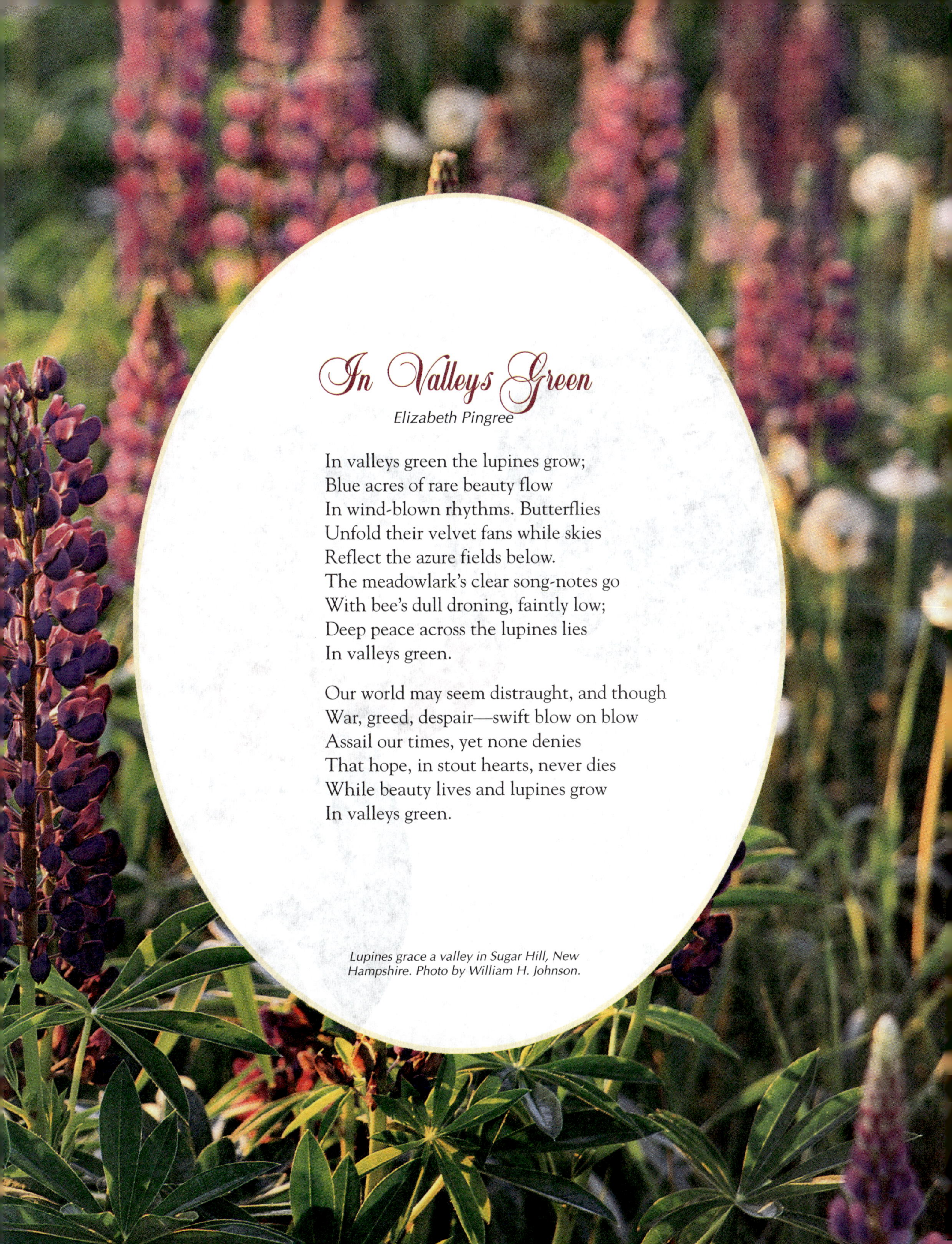

In Valleys Green

Elizabeth Pingree

In valleys green the lupines grow;
Blue acres of rare beauty flow
In wind-blown rhythms. Butterflies
Unfold their velvet fans while skies
Reflect the azure fields below.
The meadowlark's clear song-notes go
With bee's dull droning, faintly low;
Deep peace across the lupines lies
In valleys green.

Our world may seem distraught, and though
War, greed, despair—swift blow on blow
Assail our times, yet none denies
That hope, in stout hearts, never dies
While beauty lives and lupines grow
In valleys green.

Lupines grace a valley in Sugar Hill, New Hampshire. Photo by William H. Johnson.

Readers' Forum

Snapshots from Our Ideals Readers

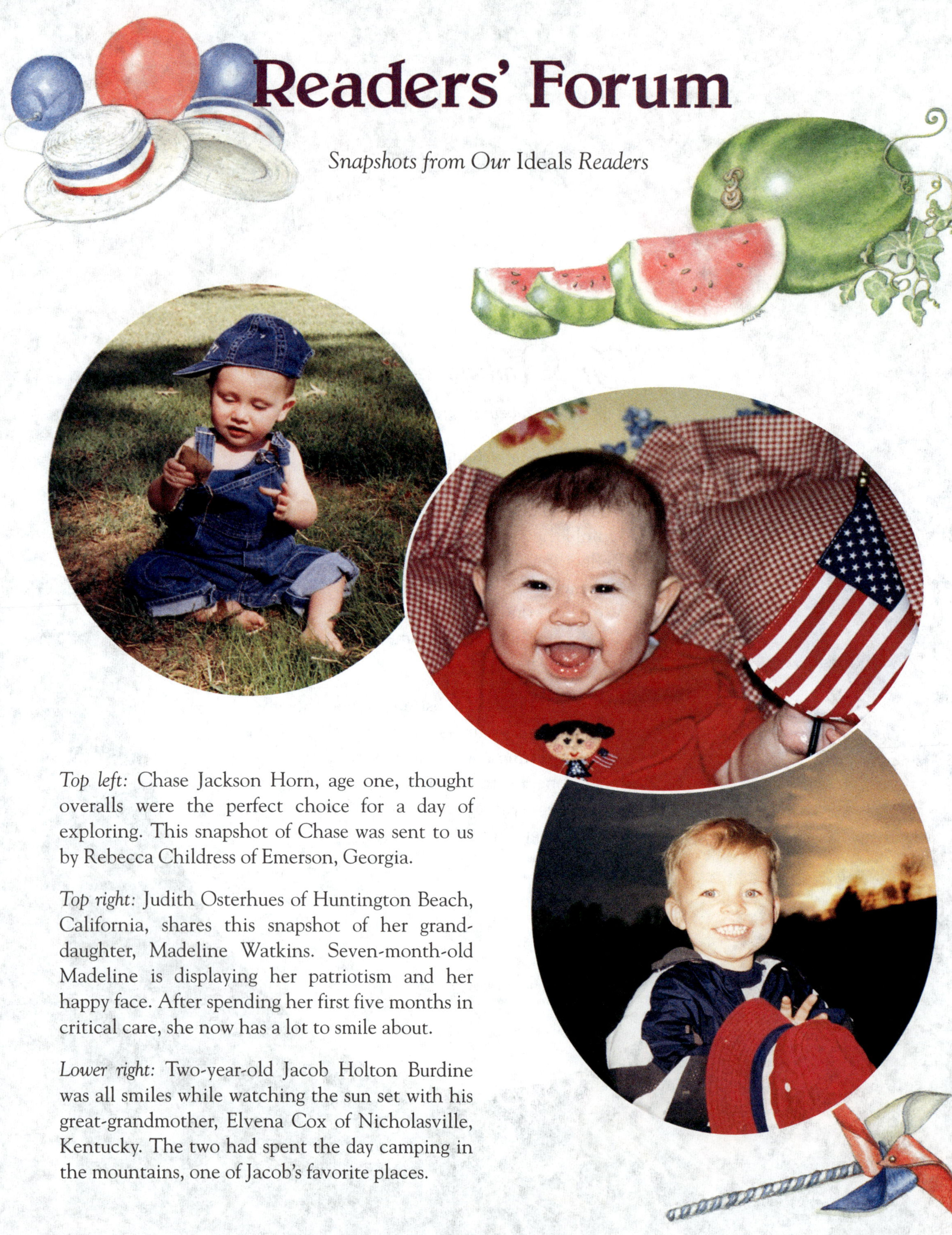

Top left: Chase Jackson Horn, age one, thought overalls were the perfect choice for a day of exploring. This snapshot of Chase was sent to us by Rebecca Childress of Emerson, Georgia.

Top right: Judith Osterhues of Huntington Beach, California, shares this snapshot of her granddaughter, Madeline Watkins. Seven-month-old Madeline is displaying her patriotism and her happy face. After spending her first five months in critical care, she now has a lot to smile about.

Lower right: Two-year-old Jacob Holton Burdine was all smiles while watching the sun set with his great-grandmother, Elvena Cox of Nicholasville, Kentucky. The two had spent the day camping in the mountains, one of Jacob's favorite places.

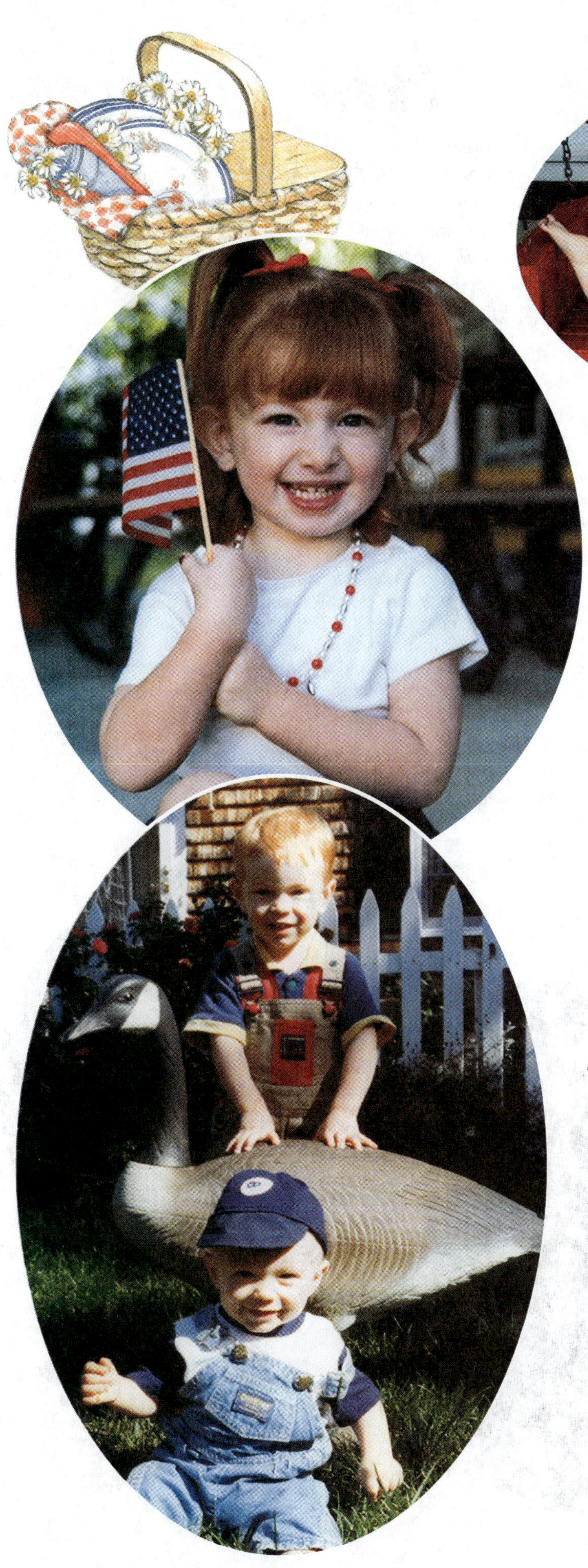

Above: When Great-Grandma passed out the lollipops, it was share-the-swing time for first cousins Cade Murray (left) and Patrick Resler (right). The boys' great-grandparents, Frances and Carlton Keys of Winchester, Indiana, say that the swing is a favorite spot for all their young visitors.

Upper left: Three-year-old Carlee Rae Page is waiting, flag in hand, for the parade. Bill Houck of Harrisburg, Pennsylvania, sent us this shot at the request of Carlee's proud great-grandmother, Helen Houck, who is ninety-eight years young.

Lower left: Cousins Austin McLean (age two-and-a-half years) and Jack Scovil (age one year) pose by a surprisingly friendly goose while on their summer visit to Grammie's house. Grammie is Diane Scovil of Centerville, Massachusetts.

THANK YOU Rebecca Childress, Judith Osterhues, Elvena Cox, Frances and Carlton Keys, Bill Houck, Diane Scovil, Margaret Roberts, Peter and Lorraine McDevitt, and Sandra Hodges for sharing your family photographs with *Ideals*. We hope to hear from other readers who would like to share snapshots with the *Ideals* family. Please include a self-addressed, stamped envelope if you would like the photos returned. Keep your original photographs for safekeeping and send duplicate photos along with your name, address, and telephone number to:

Readers' Forum
Ideals Publications
535 Metroplex Drive, Suite 250
Nashville, Tennessee 37211

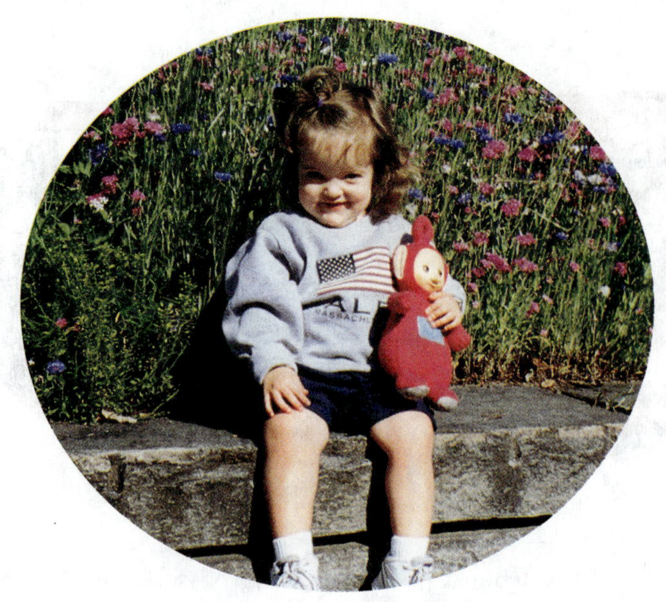

Above: Two of little Devin Maria Godbout's favorite things are her stuffed toy and her family's Victorian garden. This photo was sent to *Ideals* by Devin's loving grandparents, Peter and Lorraine McDevitt (also known as Granpry and Nonna), who live in Willimantic, Connecticut.

Lower left: Sandra Hodges of Midland, Texas, shares this photo of her four-year-old granddaughter, Madison Hodges. Madison had stopped to smell the bluebonnets in the Texas hill country.

Lower right: Margaret Roberts of Corsicana, Texas, shares this snapshot of her grandson, Chip Peeples. Margaret tells us that four-year-old Chip loves the spring and the bluebonnets that arrive with it.

ideals®

Publisher, Patricia A. Pingry
Editor, Michelle Prater Burke
Managing Editor, Peggy Schaefer
Designer, Marisa Calvin
Production Manager, Travis Rader
Copy Editor, Amy Johnson
Editorial Assistant, Patsy Jay
Contributing Editors, Lansing Christman, Pamela Kennedy, Nancy Skarmeas, and Lisa Ragan

ACKNOWLEDGMENTS

KLEMME, MINNIE. "Fathers." Used by permission of Herbert L. Klemme. MARSHALL, PETER. "Prayer, Thursday, July 3, 1947" from *The Prayers of Peter Marshall.* Copyright © 1949, 1950, 1951, 1954 by Catherine Marshall and renewed 1982. Published by Chosen Books, Fleming H. Revell Co. Reprinted by permission of Baker Book House. TOTH, SUSAN ALLEN. An excerpt from "Quiet Town" from *Blooming: A Small-Town Girlhood.* Copyright © 1978 and 1981 by Susan Toth. Published by Little, Brown and Company. Reprinted by permission of Aaron M. Priest Literary Agency, Inc. WILSON, TODD. "Fatherly Duties and Why I Love Them." First appeared in *Christian Parenting Today* magazine, May/June 2001. Published by Christianity Today, Int'l. Reprinted by permission of Todd Wilson. Our sincere thanks to the following authors whom we were unable to locate: Sylvia Trent Auxier for "Corn"; Daniel Whitehead Hicky for "Hometown"; Harry Elmore Hurd for "Small Boy on a Horse"; Mary Richstone for "What Are Little Boys Made Of?"; Charles L. H. Wagner for "O Land of Mine."

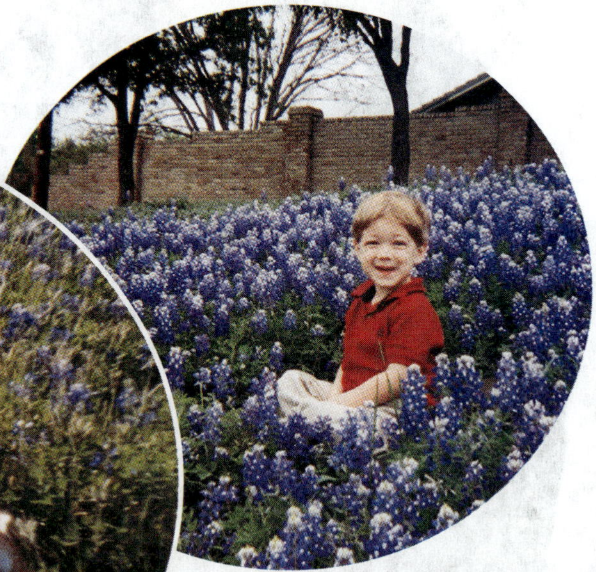

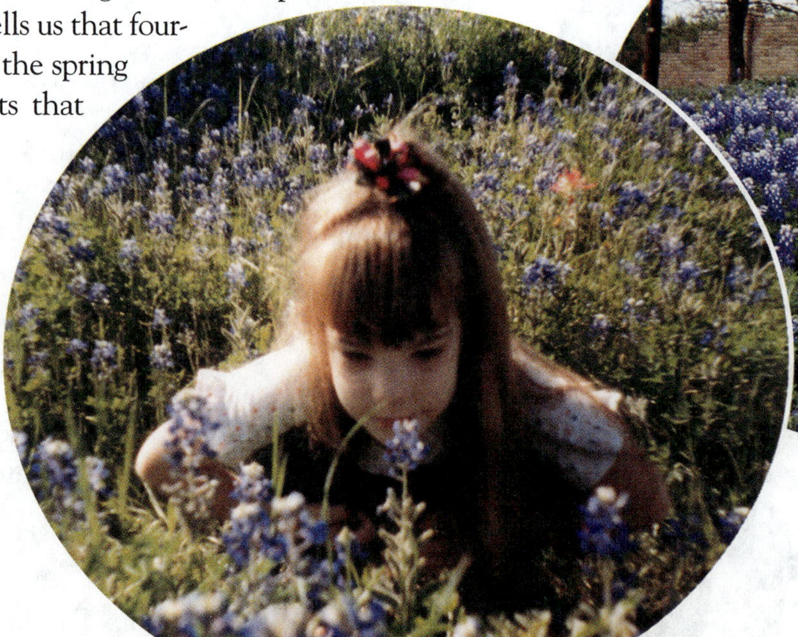